reaching new heights

through prayer and meditation

Also by Miriam Yerushalmi

For Adults (Forthcoming)

Reaching New Heights Through Kindness In Marriage

Reaching New Heights Through Inner Peace And Happiness

Reaching New Heights Through Full Immersion

Reaching New Heights Tefilah Cards

Reaching New Heights Marriage Cards

Reaching New Heights Happiness Cards

Reaching New Heights Mikvah Cards

Reaching New Heights Marriage Workbook

For Children

Feivel the Falafel Ball Who Wanted to Do a *Mitzvah*
    (plus sequel forthcoming)

Gedalia the Goldfish Who Wanted to Be Like the King

Let's Go Camping and Discover Our Nature

Let's Go to Israel

Beautiful Like a *Kallah*

Carrying a Tune in *Tzefat*

The best dressed

Color My Day the Jewish Way

All children's books also available in Yiddish

reaching
new heights

through prayer
and meditation

by miriam yerushalmi M.A. M.S.

ISBN-13: 9781934152416 | ISBN-10: 1-934152-41-2

© Copyright 2017 by Miriam Yerushalmi

Published *Torah For Life,* Brooklyn, NY. torahfl@gmail.com

Contact the author at: miriamyerushalmi18@gmail.com

First Edition — 2017.

With gratitude to

Rabbi Chaim Miller

for laboring over

the editing of this book

and for assisting with

its publication.

Contents

Testimonials

"Miriam Yerushalmi is an astounding therapist who has been working for two years with SPARKS, an organization I am very close with which helps women with perinatal depression. She is devoted to helping women in need and is successful in treating them. I believe her book *Reaching New Heights* has a lot of knowledge to offer and will be an inspiring read to all."

—Rabbi Dr. Abraham J. Twerski

"Miriam Yerushalmi has a deep understanding and a broad knowledge of Chasidic literature and she uses it effectively to heal souls. In this volume she shares that wisdom delicately with you, in a way that transforms you and your prayers."

—Rabbi Chaim Miller

"Mrs Miriam Yerushalmi presents a unique approach which is a beautiful blend of her Chassidic insight and her understanding of human nature. Her ability to see things from a deeper perspective enables her to guide young men and women into improving their personal lives and their marriage in the most challenging of situations. Her determination to keep the family together no matter what, is refreshing in a time when people are getting professional advice in a very different direction."

"Mrs. Yerushalmi's book on *Tefilah* suggest meditations that will enhance ones ability to be happy and sound in mind body and soul."

"The women that I referred to Miriam for counseling were grateful."

—Rabbi Shloma Majesky

"This book helps connect the seemingly disconnected dots that allow for a clearer picture of you, yourself, your relationships and ultimately, a clearer picture of your best life."

—Judith Leventhal, C.S.W., author *Small Miracles*

"Miriam Yerushalmi is a very successful therapist and an expert on meditation. A part of the SPARKS team, she has conducted deep meditations for women healing from Postpartum Depression and similar mood disorders, enabling them to rebuild their self-image and reconcile past traumas. Her meditations and talks are part of the SPARKS Audio Library, where thousands connect for self-help. As founder and president, I endorse and applaud *Reaching New Heights through Prayer and Meditation* for teaching this valuable technique to all."

—Esther Kenigsberg, SPARKS founder and president

"Miriam's teachings have helped me to discover the joy in prayer, through connecting my heart to the words in the prayer book.

"Since its inception, Miriam has freely shared her prolific educational and spiritual materials with Jewish Girls Unite and she has been a guest presenter at retreats and online. The girls gained a whole new appreciation for prayer and meditation. This book is an incredible resource to inspire yourself, as well as to teach others the tools to love and appreciate the gift of prayer."

—Nechama Laber, *Jewish Girls Unite*

From Miriam's Clients

Case #1

"From the time I started attending classes with Miriam Yerushalmi and using *kavanos* in *Tefillah*, I noticed a dramatic change in the way that I have been relating to my husband and children. I find less stress, I am a calmer person and I respond better by managing my emotions without over-reacting. I feel more confident and need less external reassurance; I am taking better care of myself. I now realize that Hashem is not looking for perfection. I learned that the first step to being a kind person is to have self-compassion which helped me focus on my own needs and has improved my relationship with others."

Case #2

"*Tefillah* meditation has had a profound effect on me. For me *Tefillah* was perfunctory and now it has become a real conversation with the King of Kings. Through attending Miriam's classes on meditation and visualization and reading her book, I sense that *Hashem* is listening to my prayers…I feel His presence. It is like a private audience with the Creator. Each day I try to take on more *tefillos* and I feel privileged to have this special time with Hashem. As a result, I became more in control of my thoughts, speech and actions. I see a noticeable difference where my negative emotions melted away.

"On days when I am traveling or don't have the time that I would like to spend praying, I become distracted, sad, anxiety filled and I realize the absence of this anchor. I look forward to the "alone time" with Hashem and I feel genuinely embraced by *kedusha*—it lasts all day! In the past a few minutes of mindless prayer felt like a chore, I now look forward to at least half an hour to 45 minutes of uninterrupted "spiritual recharge."

Case #3

"I describe my *Tefillah* experience with Miriam Yerushalmi as a 'cleanup of the mind.' I feel centered, focused and I am now able to have emotional clarity." I feel liberated with permission to choose my thoughts selectively rather than follow the stormy bombardment of irrelevant, distracting and sometime damaging thoughts that enter my mind. The way Miriam explains *Tanya's* teaching of mind controlling the heart, empowered me to hold on to my emotions and prioritize my concentration. I learned that not every thought needs to be important. Tanya and meditation during prayer taught me to reframe: "listen with your heart and decide with your head."

"Miriam's meditation has helped me tremendously. I have gained so much from her readings and audio classes helped me a great deal. Particularly the visualization and thinking about how to connect with Hashem and not be as judgmental particularly towards members of my family. "To live in my own tent" is what I found helpful in the Morning Prayer, to center my day with fortification."

Case #4: I No Longer See Anything Dark in My Life

"I started receiving counseling from Miriam because I had a lot of anger towards my children and my husband."

"With Miriam's help, I have been learning to be kind to my husband and my children in both my thoughts and words.

"Before, I was never really able to feel grateful for what I had. But now, when I wake up in the morning, the first thing I do is recite the *modeh ani*—"I give thanks to Hashem." I am grateful for my husband, for my children, for my house, for the weather. I no longer see anything dark in my life."

"My mother told me that she can't believe that I'm the same person I used to be, because I've changed so much."

"I said, 'Mom, I didn't change. This is the real me coming out.'"

"She said, 'I don't remember you being like this since you were seven or eight. You were an angry person as a child and you have been so angry at your children, your husband, everybody.'"

"All of these changes happened since my learning with Miriam. She gave me her marriage book to read and advised me to meditate and pray."

"I feel very good. I feel that no medication can do what all of this has done for me. Now I can control my emotions.

"In regard to my relationship with my husband, I started working on myself and as I changed, he changed too. He did not even meet with Miriam."

"Also, my son has changed so much that I cannot even recognize him."

"In the past, he would always wake up in a bad mood. Now the first thing he does is run to me, hug me and say, 'Good morning, Mom.'"

"A few days ago, when my mom visited us, my son embraced her and said 'Hi, welcome.' She was amazed. 'He has never come and hugged me.'"

"Last year his school would call me every day to complain about him. This year, *Baruch Hashem,* I haven't gotten one such call."

"Recently, he called me from school to say that he had forgotten his baseball mitt at home, and he asked me to bring it to him."

"I told him that I was busy and couldn't do it. Last year he would have screamed and cried that I'm not fair, and hung up the phone. But this time he just said, "OK, Mommy, I understand.""

"The whole atmosphere in the house has improved. My husband used to complain that he comes to a home where everybody is screaming and crying.

"Last night, I opened the door to him with a big smile because I had had a good day. I had received good news that my children are doing well at school. I embraced him, kissed him and sang *heiveinu shalom aleichem,* and I started dancing."

"My children were so happy to see this. When they see me shining, then they shine as well. It's a circle.

"I will give one more example. I have always hated the rain and whenever rain fell, I would feel very sad. But recently, rain fell for two days in a row, and it didn't affect me. I felt happy."

"I cannot recognize myself any more. It's wonderful."

Case #5: "I Am No Longer Controlled by Negative Thoughts or Impulses"

"Three years ago, I received a diagnosis of bipolar disorder. Medicine helped me maintain some normalcy and stay somewhat functional, but it couldn't cure the disease. So I was always swinging from being too 'up' to being too'"down.'"

"I paid hundreds of thousands of dollars out-of-pocket for medical help that didn't help me, and I went to psychotherapists for two years, which only made me feel worse."

"During this time I got married, and within a year my husband and I were having such serious problems that I was almost ready to get a divorce."

"At this point, I started to see Miriam Yerushalmi."

"She taught me that it is important for my soul to be able to sit inside my body, and to that end I have to make myself a vessel for G-d's light."

"She taught me to learn through three things: *hisbonenus* meditation, working on myself spiritually and keeping all the laws of the Torah, such as the laws of family purity (*taharas hamishpachah*) and *kashrus*. I started to learn some Torah, listen to Jewish music, and guard my eyes and ears."

"I learned to humble myself in a way that I'm confident and know that everything is from G-d."

"The most important lesson that I learned (which was the biggest trigger point of change for me) was how to be happy no matter what. Being happy enables a person to overcome anything. Once you're only accustomed to be positive, you're completely different."

"Less than three months after I started to learn from Miriam and connect to what she knows, I started to feel straightened out. All of a sudden, my brain started to work."

"Now I feel healthier and focused. I am no longer controlled by negative thoughts or impulses. It is such an amazing experience to feel clarity and not have weird thoughts. My brain has started to slow down and feel relaxed. This is something that no medicine, no doctors, no therapist, was able to do."

Case #6:. *"Miriam Gave Me the Techniques to Change My Family Around"*

"I was having a difficult time with my husband, who was drunk and abusive, and with my children."

"Miriam gave me the techniques to change my family around. My husband is no longer drunk and abusive, and my children are better off."

"Miriam has always been available, and everything she says has really helped. Without her, our lives wouldn't be the same."

Case #7: "My Daughter Is Now on a Journey of Growth and Accomplishment."

"Psychotherapy tries to solve a person's problems by uncovering and repairing his past traumas. And so when I went to psychotherapists to help me deal with my daughter's issues, they told me that I first had to solve problems from my own childhood. But I didn't have the time!"

"During this period, I began attending Miriam Yerushalmi's *Tanya* classes. I learned from her that *Chasidus* works on repairing the soul in the present through *teshuvah*, which changes the past and opens up a person's power to change. I discovered that I got more out of attending one such class than I did from a whole year in psychotherapy. The improvements I experienced were immediate and life-changing."

"My attending Miriam's classes has helped me be slower to anger, to watch my words and respond in a more refined way toward my children and my husband"

"I began seeing Miriam for private sessions as well to help me deal with my daughter and my other children, and also to improve my marital relationship."

"Miriam has also worked directly with my daughter and my other children."

"After my daughter learned with Miriam on a weekly basis for just a few months, she surprised us by bringing home a glowing report card, reflecting her huge improvements in conduct, learning and grades. She also had many friends come to bring *shalach manos* on *Purim* and calling to get together with her to play—more than ever before, *baruch Hashem!*"

"My daughter's learning Chasidus with Miriam Yerushalmi has made her happier with herself and taught her that she has the power to change for the better in all areas of her life, at home and at school."

"She is now on a journey of personal growth and accomplishment. I have seen tremendous change for the better. Her grades, her concentration, her enthusiasm for learning and her social skills have all improved."

"On days that my daughter falls a bit, I can always call Miriam for encouragement or listen to some of her *shiurim* on the phone together with the whole family."

"Miriam has even walked over to my home to spend time with my daughter when my daughter has had a hard day."

"Miriam cares about all of my children as though they are her own. She takes each child under her wings to educate them in the ways of *Chasidus* and help them conquer their *yetzer hara* by creating a proper vessel for their Godly soul through learning, prayer, meditation, singing *nigunim* and giving charity."

"She teaches these concepts on a level that my children can understand—in a fun, creative way through music, dance and drama."

"As for my marriage, before getting Miriam's guidance, I had experienced tension and confusion. After learning with Miriam, I have gained hope and encouragement, because I now realize how much depends on me, and I have the tools to make small and yet drastic changes and improvements in my marriage. Miriam has taught me that much of a good marriage depends on the wife demonstrating respect for her husband. When she sees her husband stumble she should respond with kindness (and sometimes silence!). In that way, she has the power to change her husband, her marriage and even her children for the better."

"Hashem has given Miriam the gift of healing by using the tools of Tanya and Chasidus to help us become the best that we can be."

Case #8

This is a story of a young lady who was so emaciated, she looked like a concentration camp victim. She was placed at the hospital because she couldn't keep food down.

After two weeks of testing, she was sent to psychiatric unit as there was no medical reason why she could not digest.

She was discharged after several weeks without a remedy.

Her mother next took her to a homeopath and still no results. She was constantly vomiting almost reflexively. Her mother heard of the work I do and approached me for help. In a matter if three home visits (she was too weak at this point to get out of bed) about two hours each she was able to keep her food down.

What changed? She started the path of prayer, using meditations found in this book.

Once she got better she stopped prayer. She came weeping to me saying again she can't keep food down. I confronted her and asked if she were keeping up with prayer. The answer was no. I instructed her to return to prayer and within 24 hours the problem was resolved—she was able to maintain her appetite and digestion.

Case #9

"Mrs. Miriam Yerushalmi's therapeutic approach has made a break through in my relationship with my children. I see improvement in how I spend time with them, how I bond with them, and how I try to remain calm despite the challenges. In addition, listening to her lectures have directed me to connect to Hashem through the secrets of prayers. I give her full credit for all the improvements I'm making. Furthermore, I'm learning to accept myself the way I am and trying to see the good and the best in others. I don't have to measure up to anyone. My job is to be the best me I can be. She installs confidence in me by believing in me. I appreciate how she said "dogs are trainable"how much more so we as humans, and that just gives me drive to go forward. She also said "knowing the problem is half the cure." I believe with her in my life I can make the true breakthroughs that I yearn to. Sometimes all one needs is understanding, and this is the art of Mrs. Miriam's work. I'm glad our roads met and I believe I'll make more and more strides with time and with her guide."

Introduction

by Chana Kaiman LCSW

"There is nothing more conducive to attune the mind and heart towards the consciousness of G-d's presence than regular prayer, where the first condition is, 'Know before Whom thou art standing.'

"Fostering this consciousness is very helpful for the attainment of peace of mind and the general contentment. For through prayer and direct personal contact with the Almighty, one is reminded every day that God is not far away, in the Seventh Heaven, but in the present and here, and his benevolent Providence extends to each and everyone individually."

The Lubavitcher Rebbe

Prayer… What is prayer? It is a journey that seems like a mystery. There is so much to be said about prayer; the experience, feelings, intentions and inevitable distractions. "But of course I pray you may say what more do I need to do?" Any activity that is carved into a routine naturally can become automatic. At times, prayer can become a mindless and robotic obligation. Whether you've been praying for years or at the beginning stages, this book provides you with tools to pray with enthusiasm.

Often, silencing overpowering intrusions to concentration and focus tuning into the inner reality during prayer takes a huge amount of effort and energy. This book will enable you to tap into the All-knowing, Mastermind of the universe — on a moment's notice. Sourced in primary essential Torah commentaries, this book is a guide to develop and expand the uplifting elements of prayer. You will learn how to transform your daily experience and receive energy and inspiration for your day.

It's time for you to utilize the 3000+ year old total experience of connecting, communicating and relating to the Almighty. This book contains the formula that was originally discovered by our forefathers and transmitted through the ages via Torah giants.

Incorporating deep insights from Kabbalistic masters and reviewed by leading Rabbis and Torah authorities, this book is a self improvement guidebook which enables the reader to learn how to overcome negative emotions that interfere with quality of life. It is a change agent to effect emotional transformation.

You will learn the spiritual anatomy of prayer not only as a conversation with G-d or a request for your needs but how to develop reciprocal energy that powerfully changes situations in unimaginable ways. How? When a person is immersed in prayer, he joins with G-dliness and gets beyond his constricted inner self. It takes trust and humility to reach beyond one's ego and think about the greatness of our Creator. This is an uplifting and total experience achieved with practice and hard work! What is the benefit? An opportunity to unleash Divine light that can change situations which otherwise seem hopeless.

When applying these prayer tools, countless people report a sense of empowerment; helping them achieve a level of security they never felt before. Most readers have experienced some sort of shift in their inner world ranging from resolving mild disturbances to remedying severe psychiatric disorders. This book is for you if you wish to enlighten your spiritual journey and gain long lasting social emotional satisfaction.

What makes this book unique is the step-by-step instruction of how to quiet the inner voice of conflict. Through prayer you will learn self mastery; how to become the "designer" of your reality and create a sense of peace and confidence. *Reaching New Heights Through Prayer and Meditation* is the cornerstone to life's balance that fuels positive attitude, serenity and serves as a shield from stress and confusion.

Chana Kaiman, Psychotherapist LCSW

(Note: It is critical to state that anyone undergoing emotional or psychiatric difficulties may need medical treatment, especially if there is any danger to oneself or others. Once stabilized, if the person can become focused and receptive, work can begin on improving themselves, while following doctor's orders regarding medical care.

Research on brain function has shown that trauma of any kind, emotional as well as physical, can "frazzle" the brain circuits, causing them to disintegrate to varying degree. Research has also shown, thank G-d, that the brain has a built in potential to recreate these circuits and that through appropriate brain training methods, including mindful meditations, it is possible to rebuild those circuits and repair most, if not all, the damages (see Appendix B).

Bear in mind, though, that modern science cannot heal everything. A disorder may result from spiritual factors, and I have seen this often. The Lubavitcher Rebbe wrote a number of letters to physicians in which he pointed out the need for people to pay attention to the spiritual elements affecting both their physical and mental health. In such cases the spiritual factors should of course be addressed.)

Acknowledgments

This book is a combined effort of a team of knowledgeable, professional, skilled and talented individuals.

Reva Baer, Avigail HaLevy and Chaya Sarah Cantor transcribed many of my classes, and helped edit them for use herein beautifully and creatively.

Rabbi Mordechai Kustiner first helped organize the information.

Rabbi Michael Seligson somehow always found time to help identify the many Chasidic sources that were needed.

Rivka Zakutinski always helps me forge ahead. Her expertise and helping hand have given me the wherewithal to accomplish many of my goals.

Chana Kaiman, who critiqued, edited, and helped me do the prep work for the publication of this book.

Margerie Libbin first helped edit this manuscript. Jennifer Schuller, who volunteers to review and edit my work; Yael Dorn, who gave me the idea about making *tefilah* meditation cards; Sara Esther Speilman, uses her writing skills and continuously helps me on so many of my projects.

My deep gratitude goes to Rabbi Chaim Miller for laboring over the editing of this book, and rendering a beautifully clear text from my rough first draft, and for assistance with publishing this book through *Torah For Life*.

Special thanks to Rabbi Yonah Avtzon for giving permission to quote from *Sichos in English*.

Special thanks to Rabbi Yitzchak Ginsburgh for giving permission to quote from his book The Mystery of Marriage.

Special thanks to Rabbi Shloma Majesky for his constant willingness to help. His critique, guidance and advice help move my projects along.

I am forever grateful to those *shluchim*, those messengers of Hashem and ambassadors of Judaism, who have impacted my life for the good, and there have been many. The Lubavitcher Rebbe, with his trademark *ahavas Yisrael,* his love for every Jew, was behind these individuals; teaching, inspiring, and driving them to give so much of themselves. He sent young couples to locations far and near to serve as leaders, guides, and role models for Jews who did not have the advantage of an authentic Jewish education and were unaware of many of the basic tenets and practices of their tradition. Almost all of the individuals I mention had been sent by the Rebbe on *shlichus.* (Presently, there are over 5,000 *shluchim* of the Lubavitcher Rebbe stationed all over the world to serve the needs of Jews and non-Jews in their locations… and the number continues to increase.)

I am particularly awed by the *shluchos* who, together with their husbands, and with modesty and utter selflessness, joyfully choose this life of *ahavas Yisrael* and dedication to their communities. They do so knowing that because of the remote locations in which they may live, they may have no choice but to send their young children away to board in the larger Jewish communities where proper Jewish schools exist (or, as may be more common now, homeschool them via online classrooms). Many of them regularly board jets in order to get to the nearest *mikvah* (ritual bath). The role models for these women were the

Chabad Rebbetzins, and these righteous women have in turn become role models for us. I was fortunate to have met and been inspired by some of these "women of valor" in the course of my being invited to speak in their communities about marriage and other topics. I returned from each talk feeling encouraged and energized to continue my work in this world, with myself, my family, my clients, and my community.

When I was a child, I loved getting Shabbos candles at the Chabad booth at the Israel March, and the good feeling bridged over to Shabbos itself. The joy, hugs, and warmth at the Shabbos table of my Pre 1-A teacher, Mrs. Miriam Rabinowitz, inspired me to commit to mitzvah observance before my Bat Mitzvah.

Mr. and Mrs. Efrayim and Freida Bloom, my first *shluchim*, whose kindness in making me a member of the family built a bridge from their open home into my future—for all those *mitzvos*, may both your souls be forever blessed and forever at peace. Chana Leah Weiner, (their daughter) and my best childhood friend—her love and acceptance literally saved my life and still does.

Rebbetzin Debbi Gordon of Encino, CA, was there for me at my next major milestone, when I married my husband David; although she had many demands on her time, as my *kallah* teacher she gave me her full attention each time we met—just as she had done when she was my high school teacher.

As we began and continued our journey through life together, my husband and I met many *shluchim*: Rabbi Meir and Rebbetzin Esther Gitlin of Thornhill, Ontario; Rabbi Itchel and Rebbetzin Pearl Krasniansky in Honolulu, Hawaii; Rabbi Avraham and Rebbetzin Yocheved Shemla in Maale Adumim, Israel; Levi and Sarah Volovik. Each of them in their own way welcomed us warmly and treated us like family. Their imprint remained, and to this day we consider them our extended family.

By 1999, when I met Rabbi Yosef and Rebbetzin Chanie Geisinsky (*shluchim* of Great Neck, NY), I had already been counseling individuals, couples, and families for 12 years. Based on my studies for a BA in Psychology and Child Development, and an MA in Psychology and Marriage and Family Counseling, I created and used customized meditations and guided imagery for my clients to help them achieve the positive thought patterns, emotional comfort, and behavioral changes necessary for inner peace and good relationships. Rabbi and Rebbetzin Geisinsky brought us to the life-giving wellsprings of Chabad Chassidus and guided us as we delved deeper into it. In turn I was able to incorporate Chassidic teachings of the Torah I learned into my counseling strategy and technique, frequently utilizing these concepts in creating new meditations and guided imagery. Without my Rav and *mashpia* (spiritual mentor), Rabbi Geisinsky, and my Rebbetzin, his wife Chanie, this book would not exist.

(Bear with me readers, as I take this golden opportunity to really thank everyone for all their years (if not) decades of help.)

All these people, as well as others, whom I may have inadvertently omitted, from around the world who greatly assisted me in becoming who I am today. They enabled me to share selected teachings of Torah and Chassidus, presented and applied in a manner which serves as a prescription and roadmap to self actualization. So here goes!

I give credit to the students in my weekly Chassidus classes in Great Neck and Borough Park, as well as in the 770 synagogue under the aegis of the *Beis Medrash Lenashim Ubanos* organization in Crown Heights, who for over almost two decades now have required me continually to reach for and achieve more meticulous precision and depth in my understanding of Chassidus and its applications.

Thanks to Ariella Benchayion, coordinator of *Beis Medrash Lenashim Ubnos,* 770. As well as, thanks to *N'shei Chabad,* who were the first to ask me to speak publicly at local events: Shterna Spritzer, President of *N'shei Chabad*; Chana Morosov, coordinator of *N'shei* events and events outside our community, Rochie Serebranski, and Nisi Streicher, head of *Ahavas Chesed* women's learning in Borough Park and on *Kol Haloshon,* who has also published my work in *B'simcha* Magazine.

Special thanks to all my very dear fiends, my soul sisters, who have been like my extended family and not only have been very supportive of me, but also have helped my non-profit organization called SANE.

Faye Doomchin, Nushien Lavi, Jenia Yashaya, Joan Goodman, Eden Cooper, Edna Guilor, Perla Cegla, Monica Alon, Mahdokht Sherian, Esther Abeniem; Kaila Feldman, Nechama Dina Gitter; Aliza Elkayam; Nechama Dina Zweibel; Devorie Botnick, Mariasha Dejon and family; Bailey Levy and family; Shulamit Kaye, Sara Neman, Leah Malekanes, Simcha Cohen, Daniella Lazell, Tova Bronshtein, and Elana Butler,

Special thanks to Jennifer Schuller, who volunteers to review and edit my work, Yael Dorn, whose reviewed my work and whose idea it was to make Meditations cards.

Special thanks to Shoshana Bander; who arranges my speaking engagements for Shabbatons.

Special thanks to Malka Schwartz who hosted my *shiurim* in her home and arranged for others to do so both locally and abroad, and for years assisted me with her editing expertise. And to Rivka Rothchild who first hosted classes by her home.

Special thanks to Margerie Libbin helped edit my work and volunteers her time as a counselor for SANE.

Special thanks to Chana Kaiman, my colleague, who connected me to *Jewish Press*, *Nefesh* international, hosted and arranged classes, critiqued, edited, volunteers her time as a counselor for SANE and did the leg work for the publication of this book.

Special thanks to Dr Carol Lerman, a dear friend, who has given funds for SANE over the years and shares her home for class events.

Special thanks to Cindy Gold hosted monthly *Rosh Chodesh* classes by her.

Special thanks to Leah Ben Mor (Laurie Cohen), in addition to transcribing lessons, for years volunteered her time organizing speaking engagements across America.

Special thanks to Leah Kustiner, Nomi Bhatia, and Dalia Rivka BenElyahoo volunteered their time to help arrange my classes that are now available through Free Conference call and Torahanytime.com.

Special thanks to, Sara Esther Speilman, whose writing skills helped edit so many of my projects.

Special thanks to Dr. and Mrs. Trappler opened doors for us when we first arrived in New York who eagerly assisted and guided me with many projects.

A very special thanks to Devora Kozlik for your friendship, for your selfless dedication on behalf of *Sparks* and for being my supportive supervisor over the years.

A very special thanks to Esther Kenigsberg from Sparks, who not only has become a dear friend, but who has had unwavering faith in my work, posting classes and many of my mindful meditation on her audio library, posting my articles in her magazine True Balance, introduced me to Dr Abraham Twerski and providing me with continuos training in the field of mental health, most particularly for PPD through her sponsored training workshops.

To my dear friend, Devorah Hakimian, who deserves special thanks. She has supported my work continuously for over seventeen years by volunteering her time and her talents. Without her, I don't know where my organization SANE would be today.

Of course, my dear extended family: Ricky Horowitz was like a second mom; her husband Al; Ami Horowitz and family; Rachel Sokolovski and Uncle Phima; Cousin Miriam Sokolovski; Aunt Zahava and uncle Sal, Cousin Edna and husband Morris; Cousin Poriah; Cousin Serena Karten and family; Lila Beychok Boyer and family; Dan Beychok and family.

And particularly, my dear real soul sisters: Ruth Himmelman and Chana Levy, and their families.

To my dear parents, Esther Levy and Gabriel Levy, for their *mesiras nefesh* to ensure I had a Jewish education and always being there for me.

To my dear children Yechezkal Moshe and Chana Leah, thank you for being you. Thank you for your love and friendship and being my wonderful partners, for being the ultimate catalysts for my personal development. Your presence in my life has motivated me to search for the deepest truths, with the goal of becoming the best that I can be.

To my dear husband, the other half of my soul, David Yerushalmi—to paraphrase Rabbi Akiva, "Everything that is mine, is his." He has always believed in me and always supported me in all my projects, in every way: financially, emotionally, and way more actually. In fact, he works tirelessly on behalf of the Jewish people and is a true Maccabee of this generation. May Hashem bless you in everything.

To the Lubavitcher Rebbe, Rabbi Menachem Mendel Schneerson, and all our Rebbes, for all their *mesiras nefesh* (self-sacrifice) and life's work.

Ultimately, I owe my thanks to Hashem for His care and His kindness, for leading me to Torah and opening my heart to the inner dimensions of Chassidus.

For all your help, may Hashem bless each and everyone of you and your families forever !!!

Forever grateful,

Miriam Yerushalmi

To my children:

To my dearest son Yechezkal and to my dearest daughter, Chana Leah.

I pray that these words of our holy sages, found gathered together in this book help you reach greater heights.

My yearning to share these treasures with you – and with all of *Am Yisrael* I hope is captured and made manifest in this book. (Of course there is no replacement for the original sources.)

The information in this book has been the key to my heart and I so desire for you to have it too. Not a day has gone by since your births, without a prayer in my heart, that I wanted to be, for you, the best mother and a shining example of a true Jew.

Dear Reader,

A note before you read this book. My goal in writing this books is to present to you a Jewish perspective of why we sometimes encounter difficulties in our lives.

This book—based upon my classes and my counseling sessions—is about what we can do to keep ourselves from becoming enmeshed in external or internal negativity. They offer advice on how to avoid intensifying existing negative situations, and to gradually turn them into positive ones.

I do not believe in "brushing under the rug" or ignoring the pain that many people are suffering.

If, in explaining the challenges and discussing my approach to dealing with them, some parts of my book seem overly "spiritual" or theological, or out of touch with the reality of your particular circumstances, I ask your forgiveness in advance.

The information that I present here has proven to be very helpful to me and many others, and I offer it in the hopes that it will prove helpful to you as well.

I also hope and pray that the sympathy and compassion I feel toward those who are in very difficult and painful situations, whether in relationships, health, or finances, comes through in these pages as it does in real life, in my sessions.

Please trust that it is my sincere intention to help, not, G-d forbid, to hurt.

May the effort you are expending in reading these books and applying their advice be repaid by your quick and pleasant attainment of or return to health and happiness.

BeAhavas Yisrael,

Miriam Yerushalmi

Note: most references in this book to "Tanya" refer to *Lessons in Tanya* (though some references are to the Vilna edition of Tanya)

Dedicated to

Shulamit and Baruch Kaye,

as a *zechus* for their children

Sara Chaya Bracha,

Avraham Mordechai,

Shira Batya,

Aryeh Chaim Dovid,

Yosef Ovadia,

and Simcha Meira,

and in loving memory

of their dear father

and father-in-law.

הרב עובדיה בן חיים דוד רוזנברג

In loving memory of

Esther bas Miriam,

Shmuel ben Esther,

Dedicated to

Tova Bronshtein,

in loving memory of her mother,

Miriam bas Chana.

Dedicated to

Malka Rivka Gerardino,

in loving memory of her mother,

Sara bas Floria Maraia.

Dedicated to

Aharon Meir ben Boruch

Zalman Nissin ben Baruch

Much gratitude

    and sincere appreciation to

    Jason Zaiderman and family

    for their generous contributions

    over the years

    that helped projects like these

    come to fruition.

    May G-d continue to bless

    their whole family

    for generations to come.

In loving memory of

Shraga Feivel Hersch

ben Yisroel Yechiel

and Leah bat Betzalel HK

In loving memory of

Rochol bat Rav Menashe and
Chana

And Eliyahu ben David and
Rochol

Who had such an beautiful,
loving marriage

In loving memory of

Sarah Feiga bas Moshe

part one

1
—

Your Soul on Fire

"The refinement and purification of one's natural emotions is achieved only through the work of prayer."

(Rebbe Rashab, *Kuntres Hatefilah*, chapter 9, page 45)

My heart always wants to come to the assistance of those in need of help, whether it be a need for material or spiritual assistance. That is why I decided to write this book. My Rebbe, the Lubavitcher Rebbe, Rabbi Menachem Mendel Schneerson, taught that meditation has great therapeutic value, especially in the area of relieving mental stress. Meditation, the Rebbe says, has its roots in the very beginnings of the Jewish people: The Patriarchs chose to be shepherds so they could spend their days meditating in the fields. The Rebbe even urged psychologists to compose special "Kosher" meditations, free of the influence of idolatry.

Both Maimonides and Rabbi Joseph Caro's Shulchan Aruch, the normative "Code of Jewish Law," teach us that prior to praying, we should meditate on "the greatness of G-d, and the lowliness of man." Chabad Chasidic thought recommends a three runged ladder of meditation every morning, taking a single mystical idea and developing it through different stages.

a) Meditation after study: After mastering a concept in Chassidus thoroughly, you meditate on its profundity, until the intellectual brilliance of the idea shines in your mind.

b) Meditation before prayer. You try to sense the energy in the idea.

c) Meditation during prayer. You try to sense the G-dliness in the idea.

d) These three are rungs on the ladder of sensitivity (*Hayom Yom*, 20th *Tammuz*).

Only in occasional moments of G-d's undeserved kindness do we get a spontaneous feeling of His presence, without any effort at all. Normally, we need to put in the work, and these three forms of meditation are indispensable.

The etymological source of the word *hitbonenut* (meditation) is *boneh* (build)— Jewish meditation helps you to build a spiritual structure inside of yourself. Also implicit in the word *hitbonenut* is the word *bina* (understanding).

The structure you build within you is made from the spiritual concepts that you understand fully and deeply.

Rabbi Shalom Dov Ber of Lubavitch once said: "It is only through the emotions of love and fear that the animal soul becomes purified and refined. Therefore, we all must know G-d and appropriately labor at meditation" (Rabbi Shalom Dov Ber of Lubavitch, *Kuntres Ha-Avodah*, chapter 1, page 16).

There are two kinds of love of G-d: One is "love like water," when you think how G-d is in every table, every chair, in the birds, the trees and in a beautiful sunset. You start to feel close to G-d and are drawn to Him as the source of all good.

The second is a "love like fire," when you think how far you may be from G-d in your thought, speech, and action. You inflame your heart with a fire of desire and thirst, and this fire burns and consumes the natural passions of the animal soul.

This is really the goal of prayer, to come to these two levels of love of the One Above, to rid you of the trappings of the ego of your animal soul (*Toras Shalom*, 19th *Kislev* 5673).

2
—

The Therapeutic Power of Prayer and Meditation

The Alter Rebbe said:

"The primary method to refine and purify our emotions is through the spiritual work of prayer. The time of prayer is ideal for every person to ascend to a higher spiritual level" (*Tanya*, chapter 2, p 172).

"Meditation during prayer with the goal of revealing the love of G-d that is concealed in the heart of every Jew, constitutes an obligation explicit in the Torah—'And you shall love the L-rd your G-d'" (*Tanya*, *Kuntres Acharon*, chapter 8, p 384).

There is a huge difference between detailed meditation and general meditation (see *Sha'ar Hayichud* of the Mitteler Rebbe; *Kuntres HaAvodah*, chap 1, pages 7-9). General meditation is like a quick reminder—it's not enough to generate real emotions. For that, you need solid knowledge. That is the only way to come to love of G-d.

The emotion of fear is easier to generate—a simple reminder of G-d's power is usually sufficient. But for love, and the happiness that it brings, a lot of spiritual work is required. In Psalms (113:9), it is written "The mother of the children *(eim ha-banim)* is happy." *Banim* also implies, *bina*, understanding. The message is: Whenever there is a detailed meditation with real understanding, you will find happiness. You will be happy because you will feel close to G-d.

It doesn't really matter what text of Chassidus you meditate upon, whether it be the details of creation *ex nihilo* (from nothing), or the wonders of creation, or how each individual creation receives its own spiritual energy according to its character and nature. The main point is that you get involved in the details of the text, understand them and then reflect upon them. But don't try to coerce yourself into a certain place or feeling. Meditation works by effective persuasion, by the brilliance of the idea itself doing its magic. You just have to absorb the details properly, and your mind and heart will do the rest.

Meditation will arouse within you a sense of wonderment at the Divine grace behind the marvel of creation. You will feel blessed that your physical brain can appreciate such sublime concepts.

In 1977, the Lubavitcher Rebbe wrote a memorandum to medical health professionals outlining his belief that meditation practices, "have a therapeutic value, particularly in the area of relieving mental stress." In a subsequent letter he emphasized the value of meditation in attaining, "peace of mind, *etc.* Especially to attain peace of mind by those in whom this is acutely lacking, due to anxiety in health, and similar stresses" (*The Rebbe's Advice* Book 2 adapted by Rabbi Chaim Dalfin, pages 104-107).

Another tangible benefit of meditation is the taming of imagination. Remember that all deviant and self-destructive behavior patterns begin in your mind. Undesirable thoughts of apathy, fear and despair ferment over a period of time, and if left untamed, they can leave you with your defenses down when faced with temptation. Daily mindfulness, especially when focused on a sacred text or prayer service, has the effect of gently taming the imagination, reducing its volatility to safe levels (see *Mystery of Marriage,* chapter 2, pp. 47-59).

3

—

Revealing the Depths
of Your Heart

As we discovered in Chapter 1, meditation is helpful
both before prayer and during prayer. How do these two
experiences differ?

Before prayer, you are focused on understanding the
material. It's okay to get excited, but you are enthused about
how brilliant, nuanced and revelatory the insights are to
you. When you reach the second level of meditation, during
prayer, it is not about the ideas any more. Now your focus
is on *the G-dly energy within the idea*. You strip away its
intellectual trappings and feel the soul of the concept. This
will lead you to yearn for G-d as He transcends the bounds
of intellect.

When you start to meditate, your first experience will be to arouse *Ahava Mesuteres* (Hidden Love). This is your natural attraction to G-d that lies dormant in your soul and is relatively easy to awaken (see *Tanya* chap. 18, p. 249). If you contemplate the awesomeness of G-d's world and its wonders, you will soon get excited about G-d, arousing your *Ahava Mesuteres*. It's not that you have really come to know G-d . . . it's just, as a Jew, you've inherited a propensity for worship.

Don't be satisfied with this alone. Your main task is to focus the mind and meditate on Hashem's greatness though prayer and the study of Torah (especially Chasidus), which will give you a real experience of G-d, and not just a quick high.

We can appreciate why the sustained, detailed work of the mind is important from the following analogy. An infant cannot digest adult food. In order for a baby to be able to benefit from a carrot, the carrot needs to be cooked and mashed. Metaphorically speaking, this holds true for the animal soul. The Torah needs to be softened to be able to penetrate and affect the animal soul in a positive way (see *Likutei Torah, Behar* 40c-d; *Bechukosai* 48b). Meditation and contemplation is just the endeavor needed to enable the G-dly information to penetrate and affect the animal soul, to make the ideas "real" enough for you, so that they start to affect you.

And that's because the Torah is really too holy to be digested by our coarse bodies. The mind is the intermediary that connects them, making the Torah's information "available" to the animal soul and the body. Many may think that meditation is for the select few, not so. Don't let the *yetzer hara* fool you. This is the key to your success. You can reach greater heights, not only for your own sake, but for your marriage and your children. So many people are frustrated, tired of the battles within, and tired of the lack of real progress. Determination to solve your problems is not enough. To change your temperament and outlook, and the answer to getting real, lasting results in these areas is from meditation. Then you will be able to say, *"Yagati UMaztati"* (*Megilah* 6b), "I have toiled and I have arrived." Our main life's mission, says the Alter Rebbe, the reason why our souls come to this earth, is to "fix" and heal our emotions (*Likutei Torah, Adam Ki Yakriv* p. 67).

The Alter Rebbe said, "When I had, with the help of G-d, established myself in the knowledge of the Torah, I sought *havanah* (understanding). In those days two places were talked about—Vilna and Mezritch. In Vilna one learned how to study, and in Mezritch one learned how to pray. I was in search of the understanding which resides in the heart. So I went to Mezritch and there, thank G-d, I found what I was seeking, and in generous measure" (*Likutei Dibburim* III page תפג and on; *Sefer Hasichos* 5705 page 12).

4
—

Attaining Self-Mastery

How does meditation bring you to self-mastery? *Tanya*
teaches that the soul-powers of *bina* (understanding) and
gevurah (strength) are deeply connected. They both emanate
from the left-side, which symbolizes control and discipline.
When you stabilize your mind with meditation, it flows
downwards to the rest of your soul, because the mind
controls everything.

Why is it that so many people eat the wrong things, say
the wrong things and do the wrong things? It all boils down
to a lack of self-control. The ultimate self-control lies in the
mind: If you can focus your thoughts for even five or ten
minutes on a single idea, your enhanced cognition powers,
bina, will support your powers of self-control, which derive

from *gevurah*. It's like flooding your system with the energy of discipline.

That is why detail in mediation is so important, because the more emphasis on detail strengthens the *gevurah* energy, giving you more powers to focus. From discipline of the mind, discipline of the heart will follow.

In Likutei Dibburim, Rabbi Yosef Yitzchak of Lubavitch wrote: "In the summer of 1895, when my father was staying in a health resort, he was visited by a group of intellectuals. Among their queries was the following: 'What kind of teaching is Chassidus? On the one hand it is a profound religious philosophy, discussing the existence of the Creator and the creation of the universe. Yet, on the other hand, Chabad teachings appear to be an emotional tool, to generate excitement for the fulfillment of a *mitzvah*, to arouse ecstasy in prayer, and love of a fellow Jew. Chabad teachings appear to comprise two polar opposites — cold comprehension and emotional passion.'"

"'Yes' agreed my father, 'that is Chassidus: Fiery emotion within one's cerebral comprehension. When is one's comprehension of Chassidus genuine? When his prayer is enhanced by his comprehension. The davening is thus the test of how genuine his comprehension was. And when is his davening genuine? When it is followed by refined conduct. The tone of his conduct throughout the day is thus the test of his service of the heart."

5
—

Changing Ourselves,
Changing the World

The Rebbe Rashab said, "There are so many who suffer incapacities, mental and emotional disorders, caused by overabundance of 'light' and a lack of 'vessels'" (*Kuntres Uma'ayan*, chap 3, page 47). Very high souls have a "blessing in disguise"; they have *too much light*. They need a greater vessel to contain that light.

If the light is not contained properly, the imagination runs too quickly and the person is flooded with too much emotion for them to handle. This could easily lead to clinical levels of anxiety or depression. The ultimate solution would be to *enlarge the vessel.*

For example, a champagne glass is perfectly good enough to pour wine into, but if you put it under a waterfall, the glass is going to crack from the pressure. There's nothing wrong with the glass, it's just that the vessel is not strong enough to handle the flow.

In some instances, tranquilizers and antidepressants aim to reduce the flow of the water, so that the glass can handle it. But that flow is really a blessing. It is your soul, your imagination, G-d's gift to you. So, to live your best life, you need to enlarge your vessel. And the best way to do that, in my clinical experience, is through focused meditation and prayer. This is the most powerful way to mental health. *(Disclaimer: see our comments on p. xxiv.)*

In my practice as a healing practitioner, I can vouch that whenever the client was willing to do the meditative work, they found great relief. I have witnessed many major transformation and/or a complete cure that came from meditative prayer.

In the classical paradigm, prayer is all about asking G-d for your needs. You beg, you beseech, you implore. You are focused on the result of your prayer, more than the process. In a revealing passage, Rambam emphasizes what is to be gained by us through the process of prayer:

"We are told to offer prayers to G-d, in order to establish firmly the true principle that G-d takes notice of our ways, that He can make them successful if we serve Him" (Maimonides, *Guide for the Perplexed* 3:36).

The emphasis here is how we gain from prayer, not only when our prayers are answered positively, but through the attitudinal shift that prayer brings about. You stand before G-d. You re-affirm His power in the universe. You become more centered and less fragmented.

As you pray for your own wellbeing, you also pray for both the physical and spiritual needs of others. As you struggle with your relationships—parents, spouse, children, colleagues, friends—you turn to G-d and pray with sincere concern for them. The sages of the *Talmud* taught: "One who asks mercy for his fellow while he himself is in need of the same thing, will be answered first" (*Bava Kama* 92a). Your cry for other people brings about a quicker response. The right person comes to help guide them, or the right book comes their way and inspires them.

There once was a town bully named Baruch. He would bully everyone in town and everyone was afraid of him. He would steal from local vendors and then threaten to kill them if they resisted. One day there was a new vendor in town and when Baruch stole some apples from her, she immediately contacted the local authorities. The Rabbi of the town was delighted, because now finally someone was going to testify against Baruch. When Baruch heard that the Rabbi had enough evidence to put him in jail, Baruch threatened to have the Rabbi killed that day.

That day the Rabbi was scheduled to travel to a neighboring village to perform a circumcision. Everyone feared for his life and tried to convince him not to travel. The Rabbi would not hear of such a thing and began his journey. After a while he stopped to pray Mincha (Afternoon prayer). Baruch, who had been following the Rabbi, hid behind a bush, and was about to pounce upon the Rabbi with a knife. But as the Rabbi prayed, he dropped the knife, fell to his feet in a cry and pleaded for forgiveness. The Rabbi later explained that as he prayed, he was contemplating that week's Torah portion how Jacob prepared to confront his brother Esau, who sought his life. He remembered how Jacob prayed on behalf of Esau, and instead of attacking him, he embraced him. "As I was thinking about this," the Rabbi explained, "I thought how I had always felt negative energy towards Baruch and desired that he be punished. But I had never prayed on his behalf and ask G-d that he be healed. At the moment I prayed for his recovery, Baruch fell to the ground and did *teshuvah*, begging for forgiveness" (Nissan Mindel, *The Storyteller*).

According to Chasidic wisdom, even thinking positively about another person can actually help them. "Bringing someone to mind has the effect of arousing that person's innermost powers. When you look deeply and intently at another he will turn around and return the glance, because the penetrating gaze awakens the core of the soul. Thought has the same effect" (*Hayom Yom*, 14th *Shevat*).

Another way we gain from prayer is through the process of self-reflection. The Hebrew word *le-hispallel* ("to pray") is derived from the root *p-l-l*, meaning "to judge." *Le-hispallel* is conjugated in the reflexive, suggesting that you judge yourself while engaging in your prayers. Prayer is a brief pause from your constant focus outwards on achievements and goals, looking inwards to see what needs fixing inside. As you ask to be blessed with money and health, you can take the time to ask yourself: Am I worthy of that blessing? Have I made an effort to be a better person recently? Have I offended someone this week? Does my moral compass need recalibrating? (Mahara, Be'er Ha-Golah, Be'er 4).

The Rebbe Rayatz said, "The sages refer to prayer as a *takanah*, an 'enactment.' But *takanah* can also mean 'repair' as with a broken glass vessel which can be melted down and reconstituted. To pray is to refine and elevate your animal soul by making the G-dly soul's latent faculties manifest" (*Likutei Dibburim*, vol 5, pages 215-216).

A friend of mine once noticed her son pestering his sister. To divert the boy's attention she asked, "Did you pray yet today?" The child admitted that he hadn't recited his daily prayers and his mother sent him off with a *siddur*. A short while later he returned and began to pester his sister again. "Did you pray yet today?" his mother asked once again.

"Yes, Mother," he replied, "I went off and said my prayers just now."

"I don't think so." She said, "Praying is not like chewing gum. If you had really prayed, then you would not have been able to continue pestering your sister." He understood the point and stopped pestering.

Prayer is meant to change you, to make it impossible for you to do something you might have done before.

Of course there is no guarantee that even after praying you will not succumb to any temptations after closing your prayer book. Rabbi Shneur Zalman writes that during prayer you might, "cause the animal soul to be dormant, but after prayer, it (the animal soul) can reawaken" (*Tanya*, chapter 13, vol. 1, pp. 194-6).

This message is soothing and validating. If you are not profoundly affected by your prayers that's okay, it's normal. But that doesn't mean you should give up hope on transforming yourself through prayer. There will be a cumulative effect; eventually you will see results. As you "judge yourself" during prayer, do not over-indulge in thoughts of weakness and failure. You are in a process of growth. Your temporary failings may just be the trigger that will propel you to greater heights, and bring to light your essential connection to Hashem. If you find that you are too harsh on yourself and you are having too many negative thoughts then simply leave it for another time. Perhaps leave these probing thoughts for late at night before you go to sleep so that they do not disturb your day.

At least once a week, try to do something intensly spiritual before you go to sleep. Thursday night is a particularly good time for some deep introspection because it washes out your soul to be fresh for the Sabbath, the following night. As you progress, you might want to begin to do this work every night, but a good starting point is once a week on Thursday night.

In *Kuntres HaAvodah* the Rebbe Rashab writes: "If our prayers are preceded by only a general meditation without the benefit of night time work, then we only become empty vessels, devoid of any inner (G-dly) light" (chap. 1, pp. 6-7).

In the prayers we recite before bedtime there is a striking passage where we accept the four types of death penalty on ourselves: "May it be Your will, Lord our G-d and G-d of our fathers, that if I have erred, sinned, and willfully transgressed before You, and caused a defect in the letter *yud* of Your great Name *yud-hei-vav-hei* neglecting the reading of the *Shema*, and in the letter *aleph* of the Name *Ad-ny* and I have incurred the penalty of stoning and the like in Your righteous Court, I hereby accept stoning; and I am as if I have been stoned... in the great court of Jerusalem for the sake of the glory of Your Name" (*Siddur Tehillas Hashem*, p. 145. A similar prayer is recited for the Biblical punishments of burning, decapitation and strangulation).

Why should you want to recite this if you are not guilty of such heinous crimes? Rabbi Shneur Zalman answers that all the little sins you do every day eventually can accumulate and add up to more severe sins (*Tanya, Igeres Ha-Teshuvah*, chapter 7, vol. 3, p. 1079). By saying this short prayer you "floss" your soul and prevent that accumulation from occurring.

After your soul is cleansed and you fall asleep, your soul is free to leave your body and ascend to the nether worlds. There she can benefit from all the good that you did that day and she is "recharged" for more work the next day.

Your soul ascent can also bring you sweet dreams. When someone studies Torah seriously or prays intensely, then at night when his soul ascends to draw forth life for itself from the supernal Life, as explained in *Zohar* (III, p. 25a), it receives fresh insights into the legal and mystical dimensions of the Torah, commensurate with the effort invested during the day (*HaYom Yom*, 4th *Teves*).

6
—

Floss Your Soul

Why does a person experience a spiritual insensitivity in the mind? Because he does not take his reading of *Shema* seriously before he goes to sleep. If he goes to sleep as a Jew should, taking stock of the events of the day, and pondering over words of Torah until he falls asleep, then he will wake up like a Jew, with a lively *Modeh Ani* (Rabbi Yosef Yitzchak of Lubavitch; see *Sefer haSichos* 5708, page 227).

This bedtime service is what I call "Vitamin C" against spiritual insensitivity. It's important to do some spiritual "exercises" to keep your system healthy. The cause of spiritual insensitivity, according to the Alter Rebbe is, "the arrogance of the *klipah* of the animal soul, which exalts itself above the holiness of the light of the divine soul, so that it obscures and darkens its light." Basically, this is the spiritual contamination caused by our sins that block the G-dly light, the sensation of feeling close to Hashem.

Of course, you may already have repented for your sins and been forgiven by G-d, but it doesn't necessarily mean that your spiritual sensitivity has been restored. The level of repentance needed for that depends on what kind of a person you are (the greater your stature, the higher the level of repentance required of you), and on the time and place where you now stand (*Tanya, Likutei Amarim*, chapter 29, vol. 1, p. 38).

If you feel spiritually numb, and you cannot feel the light of your soul, it means that either, (a) your repentance has not been accepted, and your sins still separate you from G-d; or (b) this is to motivate you to reach a more sublime level of repentance, coming from a point yet deeper in your heart.

Far from indicating Divine displeasure, the rejection of your repentance in this latter case points to Divine favor—a desire to raise you to greater heights. It is for this reason that King David said, "My sin is always before me"—even after he had repented adequately. The memory of past sins is necessary in order to spur you on to greater heights (*Tanya, Iggeres HaTeshuva*, chapter 11, vol. 3, p. 115).

The holy Zohar teaches us to be "a master of accounts." We ought to carry out our spiritual self-evaluation as if we were in business, taking careful note of every "profit" and "loss." Think about all your thoughts, words and actions today. Were they pure, or impure? "Impure" does not necessarily mean transgressive, but simply anything not directed toward G-d, His Will and His worship.

This "accounting" that we ought to do every night before going to sleep is a "Vitamin C" against this possible occurrence of spiritual insensitivity. A daily "stocktaking" prevents the buildup of the small sins, so the light of our soul does not get blocked. Repeating small sins often can cause negative energy to accumulate even more than serious sins. Your nightime spiritual work will crush the *Yetzer Hara* that gets in your way of serving Hashem. It will break through the *klipos* and will diminish the strength of negative forces.

The nighttime prayer before going to sleep mentions the idea of a "double edged sword." When we do a spiritual and ethical "stocktaking" it is like a double-edged sword that cuts away all the sins that have contaminated our hearts. It renders our souls pure and able to ascend to the higher worlds (*Brachos* 5a; *Sefer Ha-ma'amarim* 5704, p 92).

When we become a "master of accounts," Hashem cleanses us. Really, our sins are like a cloud, creating shade and not allowing the intensity of the soul to penetrate. Your repentance simply removes that cloud, like the wind, allowing your true spiritual greatness to manifest (*Tanya, Iggeres Ha-Teshuvah*, chapter 7, vol. 3, pp. 1072-1079)

As you drift into sleep, your soul, along with all your Torah and *mitzvos* of the day, rises to the higher worlds. Not only does your soul get "recharged," but all your Torah and *mitzvos* are sowed into your soul, mainly into your brain and heart (*Hayom Yom,* 4th *Teves*). The next day when you pray once again, those seeds of your good deeds begin to sprout.

The nighttime service frees the soul of anything that might hinder this elevation. If you have ever woken up tired after a good night's sleep, it might be a result of your soul being unable to ascend properly. By making the effort to purify yourself before going to sleep, the evening's rest will be so much more effective (*Tanya, Likutei Amarim,* Chapter 29, vol. 1, p. 384).

7
—
Leaving the World Behind

The Torah describes prayer as a "ladder" of connection between earthly consciousness and higher planes of thought—"a ladder resting on the earth, with its top reaching to heaven" (Genesis 28:12; see *Zohar* I, 266b; III 306b). The ladder works in two directions: it carries up all your good deeds to heaven; and through the same ladder, reciprocal blessings and G-dly energy flow back down to you.

A brick layer worked extremely hard all week long for his employer and was always paid on time. But after a few months had passed the employer noticed that the brick layer had never cashed any of the paychecks. When the employer asked why, the brick layer replied, "I work so hard that I am simply too tired to go to the bank at the end of each week."

Prayer is the time when we "cash our check" from G-d and receive the blessings we have accumulated through all our Torah and *mitzvos*. As the *Tanya* states, "by means of the ladder of prayer, all of man's *mitzvos* ascend" (*Igeres Ha-Kodesh,* chapter 7, vol. 4, p. 133).

Prayer is a completely different experience if you prepare for it in advance with some serious self-reflection.

Here are points for contemplation:

- First visualize the Divine energy that fills all the worlds and how G-d constantly sustains the universe with His love and His light.

- Now visualize your soul before it entered your body. It is pristine and clear. It has never known from the darkness and corruption of this world. And now picture it coming down into your body to carry out a sacred mission, the purpose of your life.

- Now think about your life as it is now. On a scale of one to ten how well are you serving G-d, according to your abilities? What details are lacking. On a scale of one to ten how good is your behavior to other people? What is lacking? Am I deluding myself? What issues have I neglected for years that really need attention?

- Think of five needs that you have in your life which are unfulfilled, either physical needs or emotional needs. Now ask yourself: Do I really need these things, or have I decided that I need them. Try to think back to when it first dawned on you that this was a need. Ask yourself: When does a "want" become a "need"? Are these things really "needs" or "wants"?

- Now visualize the moment after your death. Your soul is ascending heavenward, and you will now see everything you have done in your life, every single step, every word and thought. Think how they could be improved now, before it is too late.

- Finally, visualize some wood being rubbed together very hard, for several minutes until it eventually catches fire. The fire spreads and reaches a large wooden fence, setting it alight. Gradually the huge fence dissolves into ashes. The rubbing of the wood is the energy that you created through the hard work of spiritual introspection. The fire that goes forth is now burning down the huge fence that separates your feelings from your actions. Your resistance is crumbling. You are now empowered to act upon your convictions like never before.

Rabbi Schneur Zalman in *Tanya, Likutei Amarim* explains that just like when a log is too thick and will not catch fire, you break up the log into splinters, so too, when you are inundated with the daunting task of working on too many character flaws, you need to just take one or two specific traits and focus on them. Eventually you will burn up the whole log, but you need to take it step-by-step (chapter 29, volume 1, p. 375).

And do not feel bad about the past and your failings. You need to approach the work of fixing your negative traits from a place of empowerment. G-d is extremely forgiving, so long as you make a bit of effort. It is impossible to conquer the negative character traits with laziness and sluggishness, which may stem from sadness and a stone-like dullness of the heart, but rather with alacrity, which derives from joy and an open, *i.e.*, responsive heart that is unblemished by any trace of worry and sadness in the world.

True, the verse states, 'In every sadness there will be profit," (*Tanya*, chap 26, volume 1, page 343) which means, if you happen to be sad, some profit and advantage will eventually be derived from it. But the use of the future tense ("there will be profit") suggests that the sadness itself has no virtue, except that some profit will later be derived from it.

This profit is the true joy in G-d which follows genuine sadness over one's sins, with bitterness of soul and a broken heart, all at the appropriate time. The suggestion is that if you happen to feel sadness then use it to your advantage and do an accounting of your soul. Basically, since you are feeling sad anyway, make use of that heavy energy for a profit (*ibid.*).

In our generation, we are less equipped than ever to deal with sadness. The main emphasis needs to be on joy and coming close to G-d (The Rebbe, *Ma'amar s.v., Meraglo* 5746).

An alternative translation for the word *lehitpallel* (to pray) comes from the root word *tafel*, which means secondary. What we are trying to accomplish while engaging ourselves in prayer is to reach a level where we become secondary to G-d's Will. We are striving to empty the ego and offer it to Hashem.

This work is called *avodat halev* (*Ta'anit* 2a), the work of the heart. What we are trying to do is transform our heart, where the animal soul resides, like a chemical process would refine a raw material. We are all diamonds. Just as a diamond is buried deep within a rock, we all have intense goodness hidden within the animal soul, as well. The diamond first needs to be excavated, and then we must remove the impurities and roughness of the product, before it is finally polished so that its radiance can shine. As we engage ourselves in this most holy endeavor of prayer, we shed unrefined habits, and eliminate inappropriate urges, allowing our positive character traits to become strengthened. Ultimately we reveal the brilliance within and allow it to surface and shine.

The Sages referred to the time of prayer as "a time of battle" (see *Likutei Torah Tetzei*, beginning; see also *Zohar*

I, 240b; III 243a). It is nothing less than an outright war against your *yetzer hara*.

Know your enemy! It is poised and ready to distract you from your inner work. Its greatest weapon is despair and so long as you are able to bounce back after temporary lapses of concentration, you will succeed.

8
—

Your Best Preparation

For the remainder of this book, we will learn powerful meditations for your soul that you can add to your prayers. They will help you to access more spiritual energies, speeding up the process of attaining self-mastery, and allowing you to find the love and fear of G-d that is already pulsating within your soul. Your worship will become beautiful and there will be a liveliness and excitement to your prayers.

Note: All prayer citations here are from *Siddur Tehillas Hashem, Nusach Arizal.* If you have a copy handy while you are reading, it will make it easier for you to put the information into practice. If not, don't worry.

Obviously, the meditations presented here are just a droplet of information, in a vast ocean of knowledge available.

"There is nothing more conducive to attune the mind and heart towards the consciousness of G-d's presence than regular prayer, where the first condition is 'Know before Whom You are standing.' Fostering this consciousness is very helpful for the attainment of peace of mind and general contentment" (*Letters of the Rebbe*, vol. 4, p. 82).

The *Tanya* says: "The primary worship in the period just preceding the coming of Mashiach is prayer.... My bretheren and friends who draw near to G-d, and 'drawing near' means prayer. For prayer, particularly when accompanied by the spiritual work of precise meditation, is a 'drawing near' to G-d" (*Tanya, Kuntres Acharon,* chapter 8, volume 5, p. 387).

Through prayer we can draw down into our animal soul a very intense G-dly light, similar to the light of Mashiach to banish the darkness of our animal soul and at the same time extract the good within it (*Igeres Hakodesh,* vol. 4, pp. 206-207).

Charity before Prayer

Before you begin to pray, it is a good idea to make a donation to charity, even if it is only a couple of small coins. This, according to the Alter Rebbe, "ensures that the attribute of severity will not hinder the flow of Divine radiance that is to be revealed to him during prayer" (*Tanya Igeres Ha-Kodesh*, chapter 8, vol. 4, p. 142). Also, giving charity before prayer reminds us that whatever we are asking from G-d is really a kind of charity, since He really owes us nothing. You want G-d to extend charity to you, so you first practice charity yourself.

Saying the Words Out Loud

According to Jewish law, when you pray, you should say the words of the prayer book aloud, and not merely in your head. Praying out loud is important as it helps you to focus and concentrate. At the very least, if you are concerned about disturbing others, you speak in a tone that us audible to your ears when you pray. The more you immerse your body and its energy in prayer, the more your animalistic side will be engaged—and refined.

You may pray in any language you prefer; however, if you are able to read Hebrew there is a special sacredness to uttering the prayers in this ancient, holy tongue. (If you do pray in English or another language, you should still say the words).

The Alter Rebbe in *Likutei Torah* teaches that a person's soul is revealed through letters of thought and speech. Your *chochmah*, *binah* and *da'as*, your mind, is connected with the *chochmah*, *binah* and *da'as* of *Hashem*.

Reconnecting the Soul and Body

When you go to sleep, part of your soul departs from your body, and when you awaken it returns. But the soul takes some time to re-engage with the body; it does not return fully at the moment you wake up. That's because, when you are asleep, the body becomes less "acclimatized" to spiritual things, and it takes some time to "re-learn" how to interact with the soul.

The reason why we make a point of praying the very first thing in the day is because we want to reconnect the soul with the body fully. Through turning our thoughts to G-dly ideas for a sustained period, we re-sensitize the body to the spiritual, allowing the soul to flow again through all our limbs (*s.v. Lecha Dodi* 5689).

Learning Submission

When you step on the "ladder" of prayer, attempting to lift your consciousness heavenward, it's good to begin with a sense of submission. Closeness to G-d will be achieved by shedding of the ego. Obviously, there is no magic switch to remove the ego, but at least try to summon a submissive mood or general posture. This is what the sages meant when they taught, "only with a sense of earnestness may one begin to pray" (*Mishnah, Brachot* 5:1), referring to the quality of submission and humility.

We have so much ahead of us to achieve, so many new states of mind to explore. So let's begin!

part two

meditations

9
—
Morning Blessings

מוֹדֶה אֲנִי לְפָנֶיךָ מֶלֶךְ חַי וְקַיָּם, שֶׁהֶחֱזַרְתָּ
בִּי נִשְׁמָתִי בְּחֶמְלָה. רַבָּה אֱמוּנָתֶךָ:

"I offer thanks to You, living and eternal King, for You have mercifully restored my soul within me; Your faithfulness is great."

Reb Zalmon Aharon, the elder son of the Rabbi Shmuel of Lubavitch, once asked his uncle, Reb Yosef Yitzchak, if he recited his prayers *be-tzibur,* with the congregation. Reb Yosef Yitzchak answered that he did. The very next day, Reb Zalmon Aharon noticed that his uncle prolonged his prayers, lingering far longer than any congregation would.

"Didn't you tell me you prayed with the *tzibur*?" he asked. "'I do,' his uncle replied. "After I meditate, 'congregating' the various different powers within my soul, I pray" (*Toras Menachem* 5742, vol. 4, page 1804).

This inner focus and harmony of the soul is reflected in the very first prayer that we recite in the day, *modeh ani*. Immediately upon awakening, we gather together our entire being and devote it to G-d. The remarkable thing is that no preparation is required for this meditation. We do it as soon as we wake up, still half-conscious after a long night's sleep. That's because our connection with G-d is intrinsic and constant, shaping our thinking processes even when we sleep.

As soon as you awaken and become aware of your own existence, you are ready to give yourself over to G-d, because that is the truth of who you really are. It doesn't need any prior thought. Doing this will help you not to be fragmented throughout the day.

Take a moment and think of all your positive soul powers—kindness *(chesed)*, discipline *(gevurah)*, compassion *(tiferes)*—and be cognizant that you want all your soul's ten powers to be united and work in harmony before G-d. Imagine your soul powers are something like a football team, huddled up and working together with a game plan, to succeed in the plan of your day.

"The routine of the day begins with saying *Modeh Ani*. This is said before the morning laving of the hands, even while the hands are "impure." The reason is that all the impurities in the world do not defile a Jew's ability to acknowledge G-d. He might lack one thing or another, but his *modeh ani* remains intact" (*Hayom Yom,* 11th *Shevat*).

Modeh ani will also help you to come to peace with the day that lies ahead. Rabbi Laibl Wolf teaches that we only really have control over our attitude toward the events of the day and how we handle them. Your day is like a canvas with all the lines drawn, but not colored in. These lines are the day as it is destined. You can color them in pink and purple pastels or choose the attitude of black and grey dreary colors. The choice is yours. As you say *Modeh Ani,* gratefully acknowledge that G-d has planned the day ahead of you, and choose to fill it with bright colors.

אֱלֹהַי, נְשָׁמָה שֶׁנָּתַתָּ בִּי טְהוֹרָה הִיא, אַתָּה בְרָאתָהּ,
אַתָּה יְצַרְתָּהּ, אַתָּה נְפַחְתָּהּ בִּי, וְאַתָּה מְשַׁמְּרָהּ בְּקִרְבִּי,
וְאַתָּה עָתִיד לִטְּלָהּ מִמֶּנִּי, וּלְהַחֲזִירָהּ בִּי לֶעָתִיד לָבֹא.
כָּל זְמַן שֶׁהַנְּשָׁמָה בְקִרְבִּי, מוֹדֶה אֲנִי לְפָנֶיךָ יְיָ אֱלֹהַי
וֵאלֹהֵי אֲבוֹתַי, רִבּוֹן כָּל הַמַּעֲשִׂים, אֲדוֹן כָּל הַנְּשָׁמוֹת:
בָּרוּךְ אַתָּה יְיָ, הַמַּחֲזִיר נְשָׁמוֹת לִפְגָרִים מֵתִים:

"My God, the soul which You gave me is pure; You created it, You formed it, You breathed it into me; You protect it within me; You will eventually take it from me and You will return it to me, in the afterlife. So long as the soul is within me, I will give thanks before You, G-d my G-d, and G-d of my fathers,

Sovereign of all works, Master of all souls! Blessed are You, G-d, who restores souls to dead bodies."

According to the Alter Rebbe, returning the soul to G-d is not something we only do at the end of our lives. It is really something we aim to do every time we pray. In his words: "being engaged in prayer is also a matter of actual surrender of the soul, just as when it leaves the body at the end of your life. This is why it was ordained by the Men of the Great Assembly that one recites in the morning blessings: "My G-d! The soul which You gave me is pure; You created it, You formed it, You breathed it into me; You protect it within me; You will eventually take it from me." The implication here is: Since You have breathed it into me and You will eventually take it from me, I therefore now hand it over to You, to unite it with Your Oneness" (*Tanya, Likutei Amarim,* chapter 41, p. 58).

In essence, the Alter Rebbe teaches us that we ought to pray as if we were in *Gan Eden* (Heaven). When you reach a level where you are so engrossed with your prayers and so united with Hashem that you forget about the mundane—even for a moment—you are at the level of Gan Eden.

Another interesting point about this prayer is the use of the term *Atah berata* ("You created it"). Why wasn't one of G-d's sacred names used here? Why do we say You created?

The Lubavitcher Rebbe answers that "You" refers to an exalted level of G-dliness beyond this world and even beyond all the higher worlds, where there are no names.

It is this level of G-d's transcendence that has brought down the soul into this world, and each day G-d personally accompanies the soul back into the earth from this transcendent realm.

Chassidus also explains that this journey, through all of the four Metaphysical Worlds, is alluded to by the following text:

1. *Tehorah Hi* ("is pure") refers to the pure, pristine world of Atzilus;

2. *Atah Baratah* ("You created it"), the world of *Briah* (Creation);

3. *Atah Yetzarta* ("You formed it"), the world of *Yetzira* (Formation);

4. *Atah Nefachta* ("You breathed it"), the world of *Asiya* (Action). (See *Sefer Ha-Ma'amarim* 5699, page 221 and on).

So when we say this prayer we can be especially thankful to Hashem that He in His most sublime state of infiniteness accompanies our soul through each of the higher worlds until we arrive safely. Thank You, Hashem!

בָּרוּךְ אַתָּה יְיָ אֱלֹהֵינוּ מֶלֶךְ הָעוֹלָם, הַנּוֹתֵן לַשֶּׂכְוִי בִינָה לְהַבְחִין בֵּין יוֹם וּבֵין לָיְלָה:

"Blessed are You, L-rd our G-d, King of the universe, who gives the rooster understanding to distinguish between day and night."

Why do we bless G-d for the rooster? Chasidic thought teaches that on the physical plane, we perceive a rooster; but on a higher plane, in its source, the "rooster" is the angel Gabriel. The crowing of the rooster at dawn is the physical manifestation of the call of the angel Gabriel to awaken the souls in gan Eden. Just as there is an arousal in the world below, on a higher plane there must also be some sort of "awakening" (s.v. *Mi Kamocha* 5629). Are you ready to awake from the slumber?

בָּרוּךְ אַתָּה יְיָ אֱלֹהֵינוּ מֶלֶךְ הָעוֹלָם, שֶׁעָשַׂנִי כִּרְצוֹנוֹ.

"Blessed are You, L-rd our G-d, King of the universe, Who has made me according to His will."

This blessing is recited exclusively by women. In contrast to the gratitude blessings for Jewishness, freedom and masculinity, which are phrased in the negative (*"Who has not made me..."*), the blessing for femininity is phrased on the positive (*"Who has made me according to His will"*). Women are intuitively close to G-d and His will. The ego associated with being Jewish, free from slavery or male can easily be abused, so nobody can actively thank G-d for it every day. But you can always thank G-d for being a woman.

10

Starting the Morning Prayers

הֲרֵינִי מְקַבֵּל עָלַי מִצְוַת עֲשֵׂה שֶׁל וְאָהַבְתָּ לְרֵעֲךָ כָּמוֹךָ.

"I accept upon myself the Biblical command, "Love your neighbor like yourself" (Leviticus 19:18).

We say this before embarking on the daily prayers, because loving other human beings is an "entry-gate" to prayer. In the merit of your love, your prayers will be accepted. We, the Jewish people need to be a "unified and healthy body" in order not to obstruct the Divine flow of energy which is sent to us.

When a father sees his children living with each other in spirit of mutual love and care, the father experiences great pleasure from them, and in turn, he has a greater desire to be amongst them. As a result of his children's harmonious relationship, he works wonders to fulfill their requests and desires. This is true, too, of Hashem, our Father (*Sefer Ha-Sichos* 5700, p. 157).

According to *Tzemach Tzedek* (*Derecho Mitzvosechah,* p. 28), there is a deeply mystical significance to this declaration. Your soul contains within it a spark of everyone else's soul. So by affirming peace with the entire community before prayer, you are really making peace with yourself. If you reject any member of the community it is as if you are not whole; as if part of "yourself" is missing.

Tzemach Tzedek suggests that if you harbor hatred or resentment to another person it actually causes a defect or "blemish" in your soul. Just as in the Holy Temple it was forbidden to offer a blemished animal to G-d, you cannot approach G-d in prayer if your soul contains a blemish. The solution, then, is to forgive the other person before prayer. By making this affirmation verbally, we help to make it real and tangible. The mind and heart soon follow the utterances of the mouth (*Derech Mitzvosecha* p. 28).

In *Tanya*, the Alter Rebbe explains to us in chapter 32 that we need not *create* a love for another. The love for our fellow Jew is an *inborn* characteristic of the Jewish soul, on account of its root in G-dliness, which is common to all souls (*Likutei Amarim*, chapter 32, vol. 1, p. 423).

Why doesn't it always feel that way? The Alter Rebbe answers that when you put greater value on your physical life at the expense of your spiritual life, you become more conscious of the differences between yourself and your fellow. So practicing *Ahavas Yisrael* (love of your fellow Jew), is not merely a humanitarian exercise, it is a deeply spiritual one. You become closer to others when you focus on the spiritual core that unites us and not the physical urges that divide us.

מַה טֹּבוּ אֹהָלֶיךָ יַעֲקֹב, מִשְׁכְּנֹתֶיךָ יִשְׂרָאֵל.

"How goodly are your tents, O Jacob; your dwelling places, O Israel!"

These words were originally uttered by the wicked Bilaam, who was hired by King Balak of Moab to curse the Israelites. G-d didn't let him accomplish his mission, and instead of cursing the Israelites, Bilaam ended up blessing them. When Bilaam saw how the entrances of all the Israelite tents were positioned modestly, so that you couldn't see from one tent inside another, he exclaimed, "How good are your tents, O Jacob."

According to the Ba'al Shem Tov, there is a deeper message behind the modest arrangement of the tents. When we say that the Israelites did not peek into the other people's tents, it means that they didn't scrutinize their neighbors for faults. Loving your neighbor means overlooking the shortcomings of others and focusing on your own "tents" to see what you can do to improve yourself. That is why immediately after saying, "I accept upon myself the Biblical command, "Love your neighbor like yourself," we say "How good are your tents, O Jacob," because this verse teaches us how to practice brotherly love. You keep your eyes (your judgment) in your own tent.

The Baal Shem Tov also teaches that *"ohalecha"* (your tents) can refer to a synagogue or a study-hall. When you think of your fellow Jews, try to view them in the best possible light. Picture them as they appear in the synagogue on *Yom Kippur*, on their best behavior. Identify them with the good that they do, and overlook, as much as possible, their lapses in ethical or religious behavior. We know that Hashem sees everything; He knows our inner essence. As we grow in our awareness of Hashem's greatness and in our awe for Him, we too can begin to look beyond the surface and see what others are capable of becoming, rather than what they have been.

Honor the privacy of another person's blemish. It is not your job to fix others, but to fix yourself. By fixing yourself, you open up the possibility of influencing others to work on themselves as well. By elevating yourself, you become a role model for positive change in others. And since we all contain a little piece of everybody else's soul (or, perhaps, because we are all one big soul), through fixing ourselves it helps other people to change themselves, too.

אַשְׁרֵינוּ, מַה טוֹב חֶלְקֵנוּ, וּמַה
נָּעִים גּוֹרָלֵנוּ, וּמַה יָּפָה יְרֻשָׁתֵנוּ.

*"Happy are we! How good is our portion! And how
pleasant is our lot, and how beautiful our heritage!*

According to Chassidus, the G-dly energy in our souls is
both "our portion" and as our "lot." Why does the text use
both terms?

"Portion" is a non-exclusive term. Many people can
receive a portion of something; whereas a "lot" is something
which is granted exclusively to a particular individual, who,
for example, wins a lottery.

Our "portion" alludes to the Divine energy that
permeates our souls through observing the commandments.
Each *mitzvah* is a "portion" of the Torah.

"Our lot" hints to the idea that each individual has one
or more "special" commandments, that bring his or her soul
extra illumination. There is no logic behind this, the special
mitzvah is simply chosen by G-d, like a lottery. While you
are required to carry out all of the 613 commandments,
the "special *mitzvah*" that is unique to your soul is a kind
of spiritual "gateway" for everything you do (See *Tanya
Iggeres Hakodesh* chap. 7, vol. 4, pp. 137-8; *Toras Menachem,
Kedoshim* 5719, chap. 8; 5745 vol. 1, p. 288).

There is no way of knowing for sure what your
"special" *mitzvah* is, but one hint is that it is usually
something very challenging for you.

Spend some time thinking what your special *mitzvah* might be and make a commitment to do this *mitzvah* with "*hiddur,*" with extra care. See if it makes a difference in your life.

"How beautiful our heritage!"

In *Tanya* (*Likutei Amarim* chapter 33, vol. 1, p. 436), Rabbi Shneur Zalman explains the joy of looking at Judaism's spiritual teachings as an "inheritance."

"Just as a person rejoices and is glad when an immense fortune falls into his possession, by inheritance, through no toil of his own, similarly, and infinitely more so, ought we to rejoice over the inheritance which our forefathers bequeathed to us. This inheritance is the knowledge of a true unity of G-d—that even here below on earth there is nothing else besides Him alone."

We also inherit love and fear G-d, a natural desire to worship Him.

Another method is to look at what qualities your parents have which you have inherited. One of the Sages of the Talmud once posed a question to his friend: In what did your father excel (*zahir*)? You did not appear from nowhere. When you ponder the gifts which your parents have sown into your being, you will begin to appreciate your "inheritance."

The Chasidic masters point out that *zahir* also means "shine" (*Tanya, Iggeres Hakodesh* chap. 7, vol. 4, p. 137).

Make sure that the talents you have received do not remain dormant and that they "shine" and are manifest on a daily basis.

Our own unaided efforts would never endow us with the ability to experience G-d's unity; it is an inheritance from our forefathers.

אַתָּה הוּא עַד שֶׁלֹּא נִבְרָא הָעוֹלָם,

אַתָּה הוּא מִשֶּׁנִּבְרָא הָעוֹלָם,

אַתָּה הוּא בָּעוֹלָם הַזֶּה,

וְאַתָּה הוּא לָעוֹלָם הַבָּא.

"You were the same before the world was created;
You are the same since the world was created;
You are the same in this world,
and You will be the same in the World to Come."

Chassidus espouses the view of *panentheism*, that while the universe exists, it is not a separate entity from G-d. It is absorbed and subsumed within His presence.

With this in mind the statement here in the *siddur* takes on a new depth: You are the same now as You were before the world was created. The creation did not affect you in any way. You still fill the universe and nothing else exists outside you, so nothing has changed! (*Tanya, Likutei Amarim*, chap. 20, vol. 1, p. 275).

This concept is so powerful that it brings you to feel G-d's presence as something close and tangible. As the Alter Rebbe writes in *Tanya*: "Now when one contemplates deeply and at length on this matter of G-d's true unity, his heart will rejoice with this faith; his soul will be gladdened by it to the point of rejoicing and singing with all his heart, soul and might. For this faith is tremendous—when it fills one's mind it actually constitutes an experience of the closeness of G-d. This in fact is the whole purpose of man" (*Tanya, Likutei Amarim,* chap. 33, vol. 1, p. 434).

תָּנוּ רַבָּנָן: פִּטּוּם הַקְּטֹרֶת כֵּיצַד

"The Rabbis taught: How was the ketoret (incense) compounded?

The Kabbalah teaches that carefully reading the passages about the *ketoret* (the constitution of the incense in the Temple days) brings us powerful spiritual protection. Rabbi Shimon said, "'If only people knew how great it is before Hashem when they say the passage about the *ketoret,* they would take each and every word of the passage and place it on their heads like a golden crown!" According to the Kabbalists, whoever says this passage each day in the morning and evening, slowly, without skipping even a single word, and understands what he or she is saying, is protected from all negative occurrences and thoughts, you can rest assured that you will not be harmed for that entire day in any way (*Zohar* 2, 118b).

Korbanos (Sacrificial Passages)

Because we do not have sacrifices today, our prayers are a replacement for this form of worship. As we say this passage, we offer our animal soul (negative character traits) to be elevated to Hashem.

Bring to mind a negative trait in you that you want eradicated, then envision yourself without it.

According to Chassidic thought, the different animals that are sacrificed allude to different temperaments of animal soul. Cattle, typified by "the ox that gores habitually," hints to a person who is an angry person by nature, and "gores" at people all the time. He is dubbed "cattle" because of his hot temper. The sheep, which is more peaceful and compassionate, alludes to a lustful animal soul. The goat is symbolic of a colder, stubborn personality. All of these temperaments need to be refined, as the verse states, "from cattle or from sheep you shall bring your offering."

You know your own weaknesses, whether they are predominantly a form of anger, lust, or another animalistic urge. As you say these passages, focus on the traits you need to refine (see *s.v. Maamor Bosi Legani* 5710 chap. 2).

During Temple times, man would ignite a fire on the Altar, and then, by a miracle, a huge fire would descend from heaven in the shape of a lion and consume the sacrifice. The message is: First you have to put in some effort; and then G-d will respond and lift you to much greater heights than you could do on your own.

After you make a sincere effort in prayer, close your eyes and visualize a huge fire coming down to consume your negativity as you are absorbed in the Divine. Envision that all your negativity is gone.

With G-d's help, each day, more and more negativity is consumed.

לְשֵׁם יִחוּד קֻדְשָׁא בְּרִיךְ הוּא וּשְׁכִינְתֵּהּ לְיַחֲדָא
שֵׁם י"ה בו"ה בְּיִחוּדָא שְׁלִים בְּשֵׁם כָּל יִשְׂרָאֵל.

"For the sake of the unification of the Holy One, blessed be He, with His Shechinah—to unite the name yud-hei with vav-hei in perfect union in the name of all Israel."

Here we contemplate how through performing all the *mitzvos* there is a union of the "Holy One" (Divine Masculine) with His "*Shechinah*" (Divine Feminine). The Alter Rebbe explains this in *Tanya* (*Igros Kodesh*, chapter 3, volume 4, p. 37), based on the teaching, "Who is the pious one *(chassid)*? He who is pious *(mit'chassed)* toward his Creator *(kono)*." The *Tikkunei Zohar* comments, that *kono* (usually translated "his Creator") is here to be interpreted as "his nest" (derived from the root word *ken* meaning "nest"). The chassid is he who is benevolent "toward his Nest," that is, to his Source, G-d. This "benevolence" towards G-d consists of "uniting the Holy One, blessed be He, with His *Shechinah*" (see *Tanya, Likutei Amarim*, chapter 10, vol. 1, p. 157)

Here's a beautiful metaphor of a bird and her nest: The nest is the *Shechinah* (Yud-Kay), and the bird is the "Holy One" (*Vav-Kay*). When you say this phrase think about a bird coming back to her nest and contemplate all the beautiful *mitzvos* that you have done. Try to visualize G-d's name being united and feel contentment in your having drawn G-dliness down to the world.

11
—

Pesukei de-Zimra
Verses of Song

Pesukei de'-Zimra (literally "verses of song") is the section of prayer in the morning extending from *Baruch She'amar* up to *Yishtabach* (before saying *Barchu*). It contains verses from Psalms and other parts of the *Tanach* which praise the One Above for His wisdom and omnipotence in creating the universe.

As we recite *Pesukei de-Zimra* we focus on the greatness of Hashem and the beauty of His creation. Through singing these songs of praise about the wonders of nature, we begin to get inspired towards a heightened state of consciousness.

While the word *zimra* literally means "song," it also comes from the phrase, *lezamer aritzim,* or "to cut away thorns" (*Likutei Torah, Bechukosai* 47d; *Nitzavim* 51d). When we approach prayer in the morning, there are many "thorns"—obstacles that could affect our concentration, distracting and disturbing us. The purpose of Pesukei de-Zimra, is to clear our heads of all these "thorns," enabling us to concentrate on our prayers (*Likutei Torah, Bechukosai* 47d; *Netzavim* 51d).

קָרוֹב יְיָ לְכָל קֹרְאָיו, לְכֹל אֲשֶׁר יִקְרָאֻהוּ בֶאֱמֶת.

"G-d is near to those who call to Him, to all those who call upon Him in truth."

This verse speaks of two ways that we can connect with G-d. "G-d is near to those who call to Him"—through prayer. "To all those who call upon Him in truth," "truth" referring to Torah and *mitzvos* (*Drushei Chasuna* of the Mitteler Rebbe p. 477).

When we say the two parts to this sentence we can feel thankful to Hashem that we can "call" to Him through our Torah learning and *mitzvos* and through our prayers, and feel reassured that one way or the other, He will answer us.

As the Previous Rebbe says, "When a Jew learns Torah, he feels like a student before G-d, his teacher, whose wisdom he is studying. When he prays, he feels like a child before his father" (*Hayom Yom* 26th *Tammuz*).

The Talmudic warning not to rely on a miracle (*Pesachim* 64b), applies only if a person fails to pray (*Maharsha*). When a person prays sincerely, even the most extraordinary things will happen.

Ramban writes similarly that all the miracles performed by the prophets came not through mysterious supernatural powers, but as a result of their prayers to G-d (*Ramban* to Deut. 34:10).

זֵכֶר רַב טוּבְךָ יַבִּיעוּ וְצִדְקָתְךָ יְרַנֵּנוּ.

They will express the remembrance of Your abounding goodness, and sing Your goodness.

If you know someone who has unfortunately parted from the ways of observant Judaism, have them in mind when you recite this verse. According to the Frierdiker Rebbe, this thought brings about a mystical union in the supernal spheres which will then be channeled down to that person to help him recall fond memories of his attachment to Judaism, leading him to return (*Likutei Diburim* vol. 4, p. 1188).

הַלְלוּיָהּ, הַלְלוּ אֵל בְּקָדְשׁוֹ, הַלְלוּהוּ בִּרְקִיעַ עֻזּוֹ: הַלְלוּהוּ בִגְבוּרֹתָיו, הַלְלוּהוּ כְּרֹב גֻּדְלוֹ: הַלְלוּהוּ בְּתֵקַע שׁוֹפָר, הַלְלוּהוּ בְּנֵבֶל וְכִנּוֹר: הַלְלוּהוּ בְתֹף וּמָחוֹל, הַלְלוּהוּ בְּמִנִּים

וְעָגָב: הַלְלוּהוּ בְּצִלְצְלֵי שָׁמַע, הַלְלוּהוּ בְּצִלְצְלֵי תְרוּעָה: כֹּל הַנְּשָׁמָה תְּהַלֵּל יָהּ, הַלְלוּיָהּ: כֹּל הַנְּשָׁמָה תְּהַלֵּל יָהּ, הַלְלוּיָהּ:

Hallelukah, Praise the Lord!

Praise G-d in His Holiness.

Praise Him in the firmament of His strength.

Praise Him for His mighty acts.

Praise Him according to His abundant greatness.

Praise Him with the call of the shofar;

Praise Him with a harp and lyre.

Praise Him with timbrel and dance;

Praise Him with stringed instruments and flute.

Praise Him with resounding cymbals;

Praise Him with clanging cymbals;

Let every soul praise the Lord.

Praise the Lord.

This Psalm lists thirteen different instruments and musical tones with which we praise Hashem. Each instrument represents a different "tone"—time period of our life as follows:

The powerful blast of the shofar resembles the time of crisis.

The delicate, soothing *kinor* (harp) represents the quiet and serene periods of life.

The loud, exciting *tof* (drum), represent the pressured, hustle-bustle days.

The mournful *chayil* (flute) alludes to times filled with fear or sadness.

The Psalm mentions happy-sounding instruments and others that are more subdued, hinting to the different moods of life.

At all these times, in all these moods, our task is to find G-d in our hearts and be conscious of His presence (Rabbi Moshe Cordovero).

אָז יָשִׁיר מֹשֶׁה וּבְנֵי יִשְׂרָאֵל אֶת הַשִּׁירָה הַזֹּאת.

Then Moses and the children of Israel sang this song.

The practice of singing in prayer started with Moshe Rabbeinu, "then Moshe and the children of Israel sang this song." Though he is mentioned here as singing with the Jewish people, during his private prayers he would also sing. (Rebbe Rashab, *Kol Hayotzi Lemilchamas Beis David* 5661).

Throughout the history of the Jewish people, when G-d showed His love and compassion, Jews responded with song and dance. The higher the spiritual mood, the greater was the urge to express it through song, because a melody transports us from our present reality to a loftier state of being. "When G-d shows His love to man," says the Talmud, "we must thank and praise Him through song" (*Sanhedrin* 94a).

The Kabbalah teaches that an appropriate melody reaches the essence of our souls, the level of *yechidah* (Oneness). This is even higher than our external and manifested emotions, which is why song has the power to change our mood so easily (*Mitteler Rebbe, Sharei Teshuva*, chapter 2, p. 15).

When you clap your hands to a song, you purify the space around you. And when the air around you is immaculate, you are more likely to experience purity of thought (R' Nachman of Breslov, *Likutei Aitzos, Tefillah*).

"There are chambers in heaven that can only be opened through song" (The *Zohar*).

The first Chabad Rebbe, Rabbi Schneur Zalman of Liadi was once asked, "Why do Chassidim sing during prayer?" The Rebbe answered, "'It is only natural for someone who is truly inspired and overwhelmed to spontaneously sing and dance. It isn't that Chassidim intentionally plan to sing during prayer. It is just a spontaneous and reflective expression which emanates from a person's inner essence, the inner depths of his soul (*Sichas* 19th *Kislev* 5706).

זֶה אֵלִי וְאַנְוֵהוּ, אֱלֹהֵי אָבִי וַאֲרֹמְמֶנְהוּ.

This is my G-d and I shall glorify Him, the G-d of my fathers and I shall exalt Him.

"This is my G-d and I shall glorify Him" means that when I try to make sense of G-d's actions, then my mind and heart will praise Him.

"The G-d of my fathers and I shall exalt Him" means that when I cannot fathom the reason why He acts in a certain way, then I must rely on the belief handed down to us by tradition that everything G-d does is for the good. I accept this, even though it is "exalted" and beyond my grasp (*Shaloh*).

In life, you should always aim for the former approach. Try to make G-d a palpable presence in your life through regular meditation and sensitizing yourself to the energy of His presence. G-d should not merely be a mysterious force which you "exalt" and acquiesce to. His light is to be found everywhere if you desire to look for it.

The word *zeh* ("this") at the beginning of the verse emphasizes this point graphically. G-d's presence in your life should be so tangible that you could point your finger to it and say, "This is my G-d!"

Make G-d your G-d—as if you could literally point to Him because He is so close to you. This experience is within your reach! It will come organically when you make a sustained effort to know Him through study, prayer and meditation (see *Likutei Sichos* vol. 16 p. 245).

So long as you have not done that, G-d remains merely the "G-d of you fathers," not personally "yours." In consciousness, He is far away from you and from the world.

12

The *Shema* and its blessings

The theme of the *Shema* is *mesiras nefesh*—giving over your life to G-d. Saying *Shema* again and again, morning and evening, reminds us that just as we are willing to give over our life to G-d, then how much more so can we muster the strength to be committed to Hashem's Torah and *mitzvos* (*Tanya, Likutei Amarim,* chapter 25, vol. 1, p. 331).

Before saying the blessings which precede the *Shema,* we are taught to stop and meditate on some Chasidus we have learned. That's because through saying the following prayer a great G-dly light can be drawn inwardly to affect your animal soul, enabling your acquired knowledge to be remembered more easily and put into action. If you think some Chasidus now, it will help you to live what you have learned (Rebbe *Rashab, Kuntres Ha-Tefilah,* pp. 39, 40, 43).

יוֹצֵר אוֹר וּבוֹרֵא חְשֶׁךְ, עֹשֶׂה שָׁלוֹם וּבוֹרֵא אֶת הַכֹּל.

Who forms light and creates darkness, who makes peace and creates all things.

G-d created everything, including the darkness. While we would rather have avoided the "dark" moments in our lives, they really are for the good. We learn, we grow, and we become more complete.

Darkness is a greater good than light because it is closer to Hashem. G-d "forms" *(yotzer)* light in the lower universe of "formation" *(Yetzirah)*, but He "creates" *(borei)* darkness in the upper universe of Creation (Beriah).

If you learn to have faith in the G-dly energy in the darkness, then you will cease to be depressed or angry at life's setbacks. In that way you bring peace to the world— "who makes peace and creates all things."

"While the darkness of the *klipa* (negative) still reigns over the earth, you bring G-d pleasure by crushing the negative forces and transforming its darkness into light, by means of your faith" (*Tanya, Likutei Amarim,* ch. 33, vol. 1, p. 438).

יוֹצֵר מְשָׁרְתִים, וַאֲשֶׁר מְשָׁרְתָיו,
כֻּלָּם עוֹמְדִים בְּרוּם עוֹלָם, וּמַשְׁמִיעִים בְּיִרְאָה
יַחַד בְּקוֹל, דִּבְרֵי אֱלֹהִים חַיִּים וּמֶלֶךְ עוֹלָם.

*Creator of ministering angels, and whose ministering
angels all stand in the heights of the universe, and proclaim
aloud with awe in unison the words of the living G-d and
everlasting King.*

These "ministering angels" are formed from our prayers
and *mitzvahs* and "stand" forever. When you read the words
"whose ministering angels all stand in the heights of the
universe," close your eyes and imagine all your prayers and
good deeds rising heavenwards and basking in the glory of
the Divine presence. That is actually happening now!

Why do we focus on what the angels are doing in
heaven? What does this have to do with our very physical
lives down here? Obviously the angels are enraptured by G-d
because they see Him and they have no temptations of the
body. But we do not see Hashem and we have many urges
and distractions, so of what relevance is this passage to us?

Your animal soul, like any other animal, can be trained.
You might find it hard to believe at first, but the very same
urges within you which yearn for food and pleasures of
the flesh, can, with time and patience, be taught to yearn
for spirituality. That's because an animal is passionate for
whatever it understands to be good. If it eats food and
has a good experience, it becomes passionate for food. If

it controls people and feels good about itself, then it will passionately seek power. But once you convince the animal soul that all the pleasures of the earth are a very cheap currency, and what is most "valuable" is the knowledge and experience of G-d, then that animal will become passionate about spirituality.

Find that hard to believe? Well that is why we read this passage about the chorus of the angels. An angel is basically a spiritual "animal" (see *Tanya* ch. 39, vol. 1, p. 533), a self-interested being that seeks gratification. And we see here that in the right context an "animal" can be taught to be passionate about G-d. This gives us some hope that, with the right meditation and training, our animal side, too, can learn to appreciate spirituality.

By reading this passage we energize the "animal" within us and sensitize it to the Divine. We recall the selfish Animal Soul is in its source very holy and capable of loving G-d.

The Animal Soul emanates from the primordial world of *Tohu* (chaos). The angels, too, are rooted there. (Ironically, the Animal Soul, is in its source higher than the G-dly Soul, which comes from the world of *Tikun* (order)). The Animal Soul's problem is that, on its journey down into your body, it has forgotten its sublime root. By meditating on the angels, which come from the same spiritual place, your Animal Soul begins to remember where it came from, and it awakens to its true, inner identity as a force for holiness and goodness (*Likutei Torah, s.v. adam ki yakriv*).

A king is on a journey with his three year old son. The boat is hijacked by pirates who capture the king's treasures along with his son. As time passes, the prince forgets that he was ever in the palace and adopts the life of a pirate. Many years later, before embarking on one of his crusades, he stops off on land to steal some food. Noticing his birthmark, a magistrate of the king recognizes him and takes him to the palace, causing the young lad to have a flashback of that dreadful day and recall that he is the son of this royal king. He instantly has a metamorphosis; a wave of dignity overcomes him, and a feeling of royalty is aroused within his soul. He realizes he is not a pirate, he is a prince!

This is what happens to your animal soul as it remembers the truth of its source in holiness. The same "pirate" which was trying to hijack your life with inappropriate urges and temptations awakens to the realization that it is an exalted prince with a sacred mission.

The Animal Soul wants to remain alive. This is a natural drive inherent in every living creature. So when the Animal Soul understands that Hashem is its true source of life, it will also want to be drawn towards Him — *"to love the Lord your G-d... for He is your life"* (*Devarim* 30:20; *Likutei Torah, Vayikra*, p. 2).

כֻּלָּם כְּאֶחָד עוֹנִים בְּאֵימָה וְאוֹמְרִים בְּיִרְאָה: קָדוֹשׁ,
קָדוֹשׁ, קָדוֹשׁ, יְיָ צְבָאוֹת, מְלֹא כָל הָאָרֶץ כְּבוֹדוֹ:

They all reverentially respond in unison, and exclaim with awe: Holy, holy, holy is the G-d of Hosts. The whole earth is full of His glory.

As great as angels are, we are even greater. The angels praise Hashem with the term *kadosh,* which not only means "holy" but also means "separate." They are only able to perceive G-d as something separate from themselves; but we, the Jewish people, can unite fully with Hashem when we perform a *mitzvah.* And we, the Jewish people, also have the awareness of the reality that no place, nor event, nor circumstance is without Divine providence. G-d is everywhere managing everything. We truly are fortunate! (*Likutei Diburim* vol. 2, p. 180; *Likutei Amarim* chapter 46, vol. 2, p. 686).

Chasidus teaches that the difference between a human and an angel is that angels are described scripturally as "standing" while humans are "moving." Unlike the angels, you can shift your life radically and "move" it to a new paradigm which is completely free of old limiting beliefs and perceptions. Unlike the angels, you can come radically closer to G-d and re-orientate your life for the better (*Ma'amar, Chanukah* 5657).

This meditation helps us prepare for the *Shema.* While the angels are awesome and sublime, Hashem chooses us. As we remind ourselves of G-d's love for us, it stimulates in us a greater love for Him, which is the theme of the *Shema.*

וְהָאוֹפַנִּים וְחַיּוֹת הַקֹּדֶשׁ בְּרַעַשׁ גָּדוֹל
מִתְנַשְּׂאִים לְעֻמַּת הַשְּׂרָפִים

The ophanim and the holy hayot with a mighty noise, rise towards the seraphim.

The Rebbe teaches that all our public activities for Judaism should be, like the angels, "with a mighty noise"—with a splash, with excitement, showing a lot of positive emotion that inspires others to follow your lead (*Likutei Sichos* vol. 16, p. 341).

Act like a common villager who is telling his fellow neighbors what he saw at the King's palace. Imagine how animated that villager would be as he describes the glory of seeing the palace. That is the positive energy you should emanate when sharing the beauty of Judaism with others.

אַהֲבַת עוֹלָם אֲהַבְתָּנוּ יְיָ אֱלֹהֵינוּ, חֶמְלָה גְדוֹלָה
וִיתֵרָה חָמַלְתָּ עָלֵינוּ: אָבִינוּ מַלְכֵּנוּ, בַּעֲבוּר שִׁמְךָ הַגָּדוֹל,
וּבַעֲבוּר אֲבוֹתֵינוּ שֶׁבָּטְחוּ בְךָ, וַתְּלַמְּדֵם חֻקֵּי חַיִּים,
לַעֲשׂוֹת רְצוֹנְךָ בְּלֵבָב שָׁלֵם, כֵּן תְּחָנֵּנוּ וּתְלַמְּדֵנוּ:

With everlasting love have You loved us, G-d our G-d; with great and abundant pity You pitied us. Our Father, our King: for Your great name's sake and for the sake of our forefathers, who trusted in You, and whom You taught the statutes of life to do Your will wholeheartedly—be gracious to us and teach us too.

There is a *brit* (covenant) between the Thirteen Attributes of Mercy and Hashem, that whoever says this specific prayer will be granted an extra measure of assistance. Before saying this prayer have in mind the specific character flaw that you need help rectifying (Rebbe Rashab, *Kuntres Ha-Tefilah* p. 58).

This prayer states that G-d "pitied us." Pity is a form of compassion. Chasidus teaches us that we can learn to have pity and compassion on our own soul to bring about healing. The verse states, "Ya'akov redeemed Avraham." Ya'akov, the attribute of compassion enables us to rediscover love, the attribute of Avraham. When you have been overly critical of yourself or have developed a certain self-loathing, the solution is compassion. Take pity on yourself and you will release (redeem) yourself from the negative energy which is entrapping you (see *Tanya, Likutei Amarim,* chapter 45, vol. 2, p. 677; *Igeres Ha-Kodesh* chapter 6, pp. 105-6).

The *Zohar* also teaches us that you have the power not only to redeem your own soul, but the souls of others, too. When you have compassion for someone else (instead of being angry, disgusted or judgmental toward them), you can redeem the love of Hashem buried deep within them. Then, you will also redeem the love toward them which is buried deep within you.

וּבָנוּ בָחַרְתָּ מִכָּל עַם וְלָשׁוֹן, וְקֵרַבְתָּנוּ מַלְכֵּנוּ
לְשִׁמְךָ הַגָּדוֹל בְּאַהֲבָה לְהוֹדוֹת לְךָ וּלְיַחֶדְךָ וּלְאַהֲבָה אֶת
שְׁמֶךָ: בָּרוּךְ אַתָּה יְיָ, הַבּוֹחֵר בְּעַמּוֹ יִשְׂרָאֵל בְּאַהֲבָה:

*You chose us from all peoples and tongues, and brought us
close, our King, to Your great name in love, to give thanks to You
and proclaim Your unity, and love Your name. Blessed are You,
G-d, who chooses His people, Israel, in love.*

Have in mind before reciting the last blessing
before the *Shema*, that Hashem has chosen us to have a
relationship with Him that no other creation has been given,
not even angels. This contemplation arouses within us a
deeper appreciation and greater love of Hashem, preparing
us for the *Shema* prayer (*Tanya, Likutei Amarim,* chap. 49,
vol. 2, pp. 729-736).

Saying the Shema

Shema is the time that we experience the most powerful
awakening of the soul. It is the very heart of the prayer service.

During prayer, and especially during "*Shema*" (and
Amidah) the mental energy of the universe (*mochin de-
gadlus,* "expansiveness of the mind") is in a sublime state; it
is a time of great illumination in the higher worlds. At this
time, you bind your ChaBaD (*Chochma, Bina, Da'as*), your
intellectual faculties to G-d to cleanse and open your mind
(*Tanya, Igeres Ha-Kodesh* ch. 14, vol. 4, pp. 240-6)

The word *Shema* literally means "to listen," but it also has the implication of "to gather" (*Likutei Torah, Shelach* 40d). When we say *Shema Yisrael*, the message is: Gather all your soul powers! Focus and intensify all of your emotional and intellectual energy on G-d's oneness and you will have a transformative experience.

Since this is one of the most important meditational experiences of the prayer service, we will highlight a precise eight-step meditation that you can easily put into practice every time you say the *Shema*.

Step 1: G-d is Beyond the World

שְׁמַע יִשְׂרָאֵל יְיָ אֱלֹהֵינוּ יְיָ אֶחָד.

Hear, O Israel, G-d is our G-d, G-d is One.

This is one of the most powerful words in the Jewish liturgy. What does it mean that G-d is One? How is it relevant to our daily lives?

• It means that G-d is the one being orchestrating each and every moment of existence.

• It means that He sits far away on His "Heavenly Throne" above, and yet at the same time He is deeply involved with every detail of our lives.

- It means that He "experiences" life with us. He guides us with His compassion.

- It means that He is at the same time beyond the world and in the world; hidden and revealed; transcendent and immanent.

Do you want to be close to all that? Do you want to connect with the life and love of the universe? As soon as you develop a passionate longing to be close to G-d, the negativity of your animal soul will melt away. Tell your animal soul: G-d is good. If we follow His path, things will be good. This meditation is a secret ingredient to awaken the survival instinct of the Animal Soul (*Likutei Torah*, *Vayikra*, p. 2, from the *Zohar*).

Every human and animal (and animal soul) is programmed with an innate survival instinct. When we feel our lives are at stake we will do anything to save ourselves. When we contemplate the fact that G-d is the power behind everything, it begins to awaken our survival instinct. It becomes apparent that our security is dependent, not on power, money or luck, but on G-d alone. When this gradually becomes your truth, you begin to feel less stressed. You are in safe hands and survival depends only on G-d.

Another classic meditation for the word "One" is to focus on the individual Hebrew letters of the word *Echad*. *Aleph*, which has the numerical value of one, represents Hashem is One. The *Chet*, which equals, 8, symbolizes how the One G-d is in unity with the seven heavens and the earth. Finally, the *Dalet*, which equals 4, represents the 4 directions. North, South, East and West are filled with G-d's presence.

"Whoever prolongs his enunciation of the letter *Dalet* in the word *Echad* will have his days and years prolonged"(Talmud, *Brachot* 13b). This means not only in quantity but in quality too. The life of your G-dly Soul is "prolonged" and intensified the more you bring in awareness of G-d. That's because this meditation empowers your G-dly soul to break free from the constraints and limiting beliefs of the Animal Soul, as if it were set free of captivity (*Tanya*, chapter 47, vol. 1, p. 706).

Another wonderfully insightful teaching of Chasidus sheds meaning on the term *echad*, by comparing it with a similar Hebrew word, *yachid*. *Yachid* means "one" in the sense of the singular, solitary one. *Echad* implies a unity of disparate parts, a coming together and oneness in a place of diversity. So when we say G-d is *echad*, it means that we can see G-d in the different facets of the world. In all the spiritual strata and down here in the physical realm, His oneness pervades all.

Step 2: G-d within the World

בָּרוּךְ שֵׁם כְּבוֹד מַלְכוּתוֹ לְעוֹלָם וָעֶד.

Blessed be the name of His honorable kingdom forever and ever!

Here we focus our thoughts to how G-d's presence is to be found within the world. When you see a tree, a bird, or people doing their work, or hear a beautiful piece of music, or taste wonderful food — it is all a manifestation of G-d. In Chasidic lexicon this awareness is called *memaleh kol almin* (He-fills-all-worlds). This meditation is so powerful because it makes your relationship with G-d real and concrete.

In one of his travels, Rabbi Shneur Zalman of Liadi passed through the town of Zhebarahev. A widow lifted her two small children onto the Rebbe's wagon so that he might bless them.

One of the children, a five year old boy called Yisrolik, asked Rabbi Shneur Zalman: "How after reciting the first verse of the *Shema*, contemplating G-d's oneness, are we able to return back to this world and say, "Love the Lord your G-d with all your heart and all your soul'?"

Rabbi Shneur Zalman replied: "Because in the middle we say 'Blessed be the name of the glory of His kingdom forever and ever," meditating on how G-d is present in the world and that you don't need to leave the world to find Him."

When Rabbi Shneur Zalman returned to his home in Liozna he approached his students and said, "Chassidim! A small child asked me a question which none of you thought to ask!"

That boy, "Yisrolik," was later to become the great Rabbi Yisroel of Ruzhin.

Rabbi Nachman teaches us that the verse of *Shema* as well as the six words of the sentence that follows, "Blessed be the Name of His glorious kingdom for ever and ever," total twelve words, corresponding to the twelve tribes. When we say these twelve words we are linking our soul to all of the twelve tribes, and thereby to the entire Jewish people.

Step 3: Your Two Hearts

וְאָהַבְתָּ אֵת יְיָ אֱלֹהֶיךָ בְּכָל לְבָבְךָ,
וּבְכָל נַפְשְׁךָ, וּבְכָל מְאֹדֶךָ.

And you shall love G-d your G-d with all your heart, and with all your soul, and with all your might.

The word *levavcha* is written in the plural (literally "your hearts"), to remind us that we have two impulses, the animal and the G-dly (*Rashi, Va'eschanan* 6:5), and both of them can be harmonized to worship G-d together.

Now start to feel love of G-d and visualize both of your hearts.

The spiritual work of prayer gradually brings about a fiery love for G-d and burns away negativity. The goodness that is within the animal soul needs to be brought out, just like the fire is needed to remove impurities. With each prayer you begin to teach the animal soul to want what G-d wants, and you will slowly begin to receive extra strength from Hashem in your efforts to get close to Him. And when you make the effort to meditate on G-d, you will naturally come to love Him (*Igeres Ha-Kodesh*, chapter 12, vol. 4, p. 207).

The *Baal Shem Tov* taught that the numerical value of *VeAhavta* ("And you shall love") is twice the value of *ohr* ("light"). This in turn is the numerical equivalent of *raz* ("secret"), whose mirror image is *zar* ("an alien"), (*Keser Shem Tov, Hosafos* p. 24).

The message here is that we should take that which seems to be alien to G-d, and uncover its secret, hidden spark of light. Everything ultimately has a purpose for the good. Your challenge is to find it. The word light has its numerical value doubled alluding to two ways that light can be revealed: *or yashar* ("direct light") and *or chozer* ("reflected light"). Sometimes the positive outcome of an event is obvious and direct. But on other occasions you only realize why G-d led you on a certain path in hindsight. Events which at the time seemed like misfortune, brought you later to greater heights. This is the meaning of "reflected light." So everything that happens is a form of light: the question is just whether it is direct or reflected.

The Maggid of Mezritch asked: How can we be commanded to love G-d? It is not within a human being's power to simply switch on or off the emotion of love? What the Torah means, the Rambam explained, when it tells us to love G-d is to think about Him so much that we come to love Him. You can't choose what you will love, but you do have the power to focus your mind on whatever you please. If you think about the wonder of G-d enough, you will come to love Him (See *Derech Mitzvotecha* 199a; Rambam, *Hilchot Yesodei HaTorah* chap. 2).

"If one prays and suddenly his heart is filled with a surge of joy and love for G-d, he should understand that G-d has chosen to fulfill his wishes, as it says: 'And find delight in Hashem, and He will grant you the desires of your heart' (Psalms 37:4). If one experiences a surge of ecstasy at any time of day or night—not during prayers—he should cherish this precious moment and remain silent as the intensity of his feelings subsides. These wonderful moments of passionate Divine love are similar to the revelations of the prophets of old. The experience is other-worldly" (Sefer Chassidim section 773).

וּבְכָל נַפְשְׁךָ.

And with all your soul.

Loving G-d with all of your soul means that your love is so intense that all the "departments" of the soul—raw intellect and emotions, and the powers of thought, speech and deed—are devoted to G-d.

It is also a declaration of faith, that you would be willing to give your life for G-d, if necessary.

Deep in our souls we can all find the point where we would die for G-d. The willingness to do this provides the emotional foundation to worship Him fully, with all the devotion that we can muster. In the words of the Alter Rebbe, "but because the fulfillment of the Torah and its commandments is contingent on being constantly aware of your readiness to surrender your life to G-d for the sake of His unity, if the situation would warrant it." This is the message contained in the *Shema*. "He must therefore recite it twice daily, morning and evening, so that this awareness will be fixed permanently in your heart, and will not depart from His memory night and day. In this way, one is able to withstand his Evil Inclination and to vanquish it at every time and every moment" (*Tanya, Likutei Amarim,* chap. 25, vol. 1, p. 341).

וּבְכָל מְאֹדֶךָ.

With all your might.

When we get to the phrase "with all your might" (*be-chol me'odecha*) in the *Shema* prayer we can think:

1.) *Me'odecha* refers to the might that the *neshama* of a Jew has to serve Hashem faithfully, so much so that it is ready to sacrifice its life for Hashem. And since we are equipped to surrender our lives for G-d, in order not to be G-d forbid separated from Him, all the more so we are equipped with this might to do G-d's will, even that which "seems" difficult to us.

2.) The elevation of spiritual sparks is accomplished mainly by our prayers. For our prayers are uniquely able to draw down infinite degrees of G-dliness. Prayer alone can bring about changes in the world. In fact, the Alter Rebbe teaches that no other *mitzvah* has the power to change reality—bringing rain, income, health, and most importantly to change your animal soul —like prayer (*Tanya, Kuntres Acharon,* p. 155 in Vilna ed.).

3.) In Hebrew, the word *me-od* ("might"), can be re-arranged to spell *adam* ("man"). While there are many words for "man" in Hebrew, the term *adam* implies a more elevated form of human existence associated with *mochin de-gadlus,* an expansiveness of mind. We are attempting to worship G-d in our highest, most actualized state of being (*Ma'amarim* of *Tzemach Tzedek,* 5615 p. 114).

Step 4: Second Paragraph of *Shema*

וְנָתַתִּי מְטַר | אַרְצְכֶם בְּעִתּוֹ, יוֹרֶה וּמַלְקוֹשׁ, וְאָסַפְתָּ
דְגָנֶךָ וְתִירֹשְׁךָ וְיִצְהָרֶךָ: וְנָתַתִּי עֵשֶׂב | בְּשָׂדְךָ לִבְהֶמְתֶּךָ,

וְאָכַלְתָּ וְשָׂבָעְתָּ... יְמֵיכֶם וִימֵי בְנֵיכֶם | עַל הָאֲדָמָה אֲשֶׁר נִשְׁבַּע | יְיָ לַאֲבֹתֵיכֶם לָתֵת לָהֶם, כִּימֵי הַשָּׁמַיִם | עַל הָאָרֶץ.

"I will give the rain of your land in its season, the first rains and the last rains, so that you can gather in your grain, your wine, and your oil; and I will give grass in your field for your cattle; you will eat and you will be satisfied... your days, and the days of your children, will be numerous, on the land which G-d swore to your fathers, to give them, just like the skies remain above the earth."

The sprouting of those seeds of love from your meditation are now creating a stronger mind for you. Like the sprouting of a seed, your heart is glowing stronger with love and fear of G-d. The produce of your sprouting mind will be healthy positive emotions.

This most deep worship, done with *kavanah* and with attentive care, will result with blessings from G-d. *"And it shall come to pass, if you will diligently obey... you will eat and you will be satisfied."* You will meditate and it will result in love and fear of G-d.

But if your worship is done without *kavanah*, without being taken to heart, then your worship will not "yield its harvest." There will be "clouds and wind, but no rain." There will be arrogance and coarseness of spirit — but no real, practical results. You will still wait for your personal redemption, G-d forbid.

Step 5: Third Paragraph of *Shema*

וְלֹא תָתוּרוּ אַחֲרֵי לְבַבְכֶם וְאַחֲרֵי
עֵינֵיכֶם, אֲשֶׁר אַתֶּם זֹנִים אַחֲרֵיהֶם.

And you will not follow after your heart and your own eyes, which lead you astray.

After the spiritual work of the *Shema*, you will have strengthened your ability not to not go after your heart's urges. Visualize how you are able to not go after these negative emotions. See yourself being in control. Your heart's urges might include anger, anxiety and worry. These urges manifest themselves in the left side of the heart, the seat of the animal soul. Your heart will try to take over your mind, but you must not let it succeed! You will achieve mastery over the heart

Many people think, "My heart is who I am. I can't easily change. I speak from my heart, because that is what comes naturally." But we have been commanded by the Torah not to succumb to our heart's urges. G-d knows we can be successful in this task. We all have an inborn capacity to train our heart to be disciplined.

Don't think too much how daunting the task ahead seems. Begin today, and just start from the beginning. Be disciplined about doing your work day by day and you will have the strength to succeed in having more mastery over your heart.

Most people think that the command "not to follow after your heart" refers only to indulgence in material pleasures. But the Torah is telling us not to follow our negative moods too. "Do not follow after your heart," when it tells you to be sad, anxious or negative.

Having negative thoughts is normal, since they arise from the *yetzer hara,* and usually not something you can control. But what you can master is the technique of ridding yourself of these thoughts as soon as they occur. After the thought occurs to you, you do have the free will to rid yourself of it by diverting your mind to something else. This, says the Alter Rebbe, brings G-dliness to this world and great joy to Hashem.

"You should not feel depressed and troubled at heart, even if you are busy all your life in this conflict with the thoughts which will always enter your mind. For perhaps that is what you were created for, and this is the service that is demanded of you—to subdue the negative forces constantly" (*Tanya,* chapter 27, volume 1, p. 357).

If you follow the Alter Rebbe's advice and struggle with your *yezter hara* your entire life, you may not become perfectly "holy," as in "saintly," but you will be "holy" (*kadosh*), in another sense. *Kadosh* also means "removed," or "separate," and you will be "separate" from the negativity of your Animal Soul. G-d will definitely free you from your negative tendencies in return for the effort that you made (see *Tanya,* chap. 27, volume 1, p. 364).

Step 6: Concluding the Third Paragraph of *Shema*

וִהְיִיתֶם קְדֹשִׁים לֵאלֹהֵיכֶם.

And you will be holy to your G-d.

Now, because you made the effort, G-d is endowing you with holiness. That makes it easier for you to submit to His will.

G-d's fire is melting away your negativity and His holy energy is redeeming you.

Visualize yourself as perfectly holy, without negativity.

Step 7: Leaving Egypt

אֲנִי יְיָ אֱלֹהֵיכֶם, אֲשֶׁר הוֹצֵאתִי אֶתְכֶם מֵאֶרֶץ מִצְרָיִם.

I am the L-rd your G-d who took you out of Egypt.

In Chassidic thought, Egypt (*Mitzrayim*) is symbolic of limiting beliefs, thoughts that prevent us from positive activity and growth. The fear of failure, the feeling of shame and low self-esteem and the tendency to procrastinate, all arise from limiting beliefs. As we recite the third paragraph of *Shema*, which depicts the historical/geographical departure from Egypt, it is time to challenge some of your limiting beliefs and free yourself from the personal/psychological *Mitzrayim* (*Tanya*, chapter 47, vol. 2, p. 706; *Ma'amar s.v. b'chol dor* 5734).

Visualize your own personal *Yetziat Mitzrayim*, how G-d has helped you to free yourself from your negativity.

He is bringing you out of your limitations, and you are doing your part. Your efforts in prayer is what will lead you to the real you.

The Alter Rebbe teaches us that every day when we pray, we are leaving Egypt (limiting thoughts) anew. Our G-dly soul is actually departing its exile from the animal soul's captivity. Every day we must see ourselves as if we today we left *mitzrayim* (see *Tanya*, ibid.)

If a young boy puts on his clothes of even a year ago, onlookers will think something is wrong with the boy. Doesn't he realizes that his clothes don't fit him anymore? People might think he was mentally challenged. Well, everyday our soul, too, has a growth spurt. So today my "clothes" of my soul, (that is my thought speech and action in Torah and *mitzvos*) have to match the state of my more elevated soul.

Step 8: The Last Word

אֱמֶת.

True.

You have arrived. You are free to be the real you.

Imagine that!

The Rebbe *Rashab* teaches us that when we reach this word after having said *Shema*, our G-dly soul now is completely freed from the exile of animal soul (*Kuntres HaAvodah*, chap. 5, p. 138).

So now let's recap the eight steps that are hidden in the *shema* that you can take toward your own personal redemption *(geula)*.

Remember these key words

1) *Echad* - in the first sentence of *Shema*.

Meditate on G-dliness beyond the world.

2) *Baruch Shem Kevod* (second sentence of *shema*).

Meditate on G-dliness within the world.

The more detailed your meditation is the more you will get to a greater love of Hashem.

Then... 3) *Bechol levavcha.*

Meditate that both your hearts now (including your animal soul's heart) love Hashem.

Then... 4) *Adama titein yevula.*

Meditate that your intellect will yield produce of healthy positive emotions by developing intellectual wherewithal.

Then... 5) *Lo TaTuru.*

Meditate now that you are more intellectually minded you will be less tempted to go after your heart's desire; that is, not only your lustful heart's desire but also your negative emotions.

Then... 6) *Vehayitem kedoshim.*

Meditate that G-d will separate you from your dark side.

Then... 7) *Mitzrayim.*

Meditate that G-d now will take you out of your own Exile for your efforts of not going after your heart's desires.

Then... 8) *Emes.*

Meditate that you have arrived to the truth of you.

Then.... You are finally free!

Meditation on G-d's Presence

This is a wonderful meditation to carry out in Step 2, when we muse on G-d's presence in the world. In this meditation we are going to journey through the Four Kingdoms of Mineral, Vegetable, Animal and Human, and try to imaginatively visualize the *memaleh kol olamin* energy in each one.

1) Choose one example from each kingdom and identify its name in Hebrew, for example Mineral: earth *(adama)*, Vegetable: carrot *(gezer)*; Animal: bird *(tzipor)*. For the Human kingdom you could use your own Hebrew name.

2) Slowly contemplate and visualize each of the creations that you have chosen and visualize the Hebrew letters of their name. E.g., first picture the earth and then visualize the word אדמה in Hebrew.

3) As you see the Hebrew letters of that kingdom your goal is to try to capture a feeling and understanding of the spiritual life force that enlivens it. The life force is conveyed by the Hebrew letters that form its name. Take plenty of time to explore and visualize all four kingdoms.

4) Now focus on a particular physical quality of each category, e.g. the color of an item, and start to feel the spiritual mood or emotion that the thing emanates.

5) Finally, move through each of the four kingdoms and contemplate each of your chosen items in its primordial

form, before being created, how it existed in unformed potential.

(This will take some use of the imagination. But remember, it will be extremely valuable to you to develop your imagination for good and holy things. If the imagination is left to its own devices, it will only help the *yezter hara* to run wild, and that is the root of many psychological disorders).

What if, despite all your efforts in meditating on G-d's greatness, you don't become excited and aroused emotionally?

The Alter Rebbe answers that if the love and fear born from your meditation remain "stuck" in your mind and the depths of your heart, it's not a cause for concern. G-d will "join the thought to the deed" (*Kidushin* 40a), and ensure that the results of your meditation will still permeate your *mitzvah* observance, just as if your emotions have been open and aroused (*Tanya, Likutei Amarim* chapter 16, vol. 1, p. 235).

13

The *Shemoneh Esrei / Amida*

During the reading of the *Shema* you verbally declare your willingness to worship G-d when you say, *Hashem Echad* "G-d is One." During the *Amida*, the "standing prayer," you have a chance to demonstrate that dedication physically with your body, when you bow in four times devotion before G-d.

When you pray, you also elevate the energy that you have absorbed through eating and drinking, as well as all the energy that you put into earning a living. It all becomes a vehicle for G-dliness through prayer (*Tanya, Likutei Amarim* chap. 34, vol. 2, p. 448).

סוֹמֵךְ נוֹפְלִים, וְרוֹפֵא חוֹלִים, וּמַתִּיר אֲסוּרִים.

You support the falling, heal the sick, loosen the bound.

This is reference to the falling of the *Shechina* (Divine Presence). It is phrased in the plural, alluding to many organs of the spiritual "body" of the Jewish people, which are the "organs" of the *Shechina*.

The *Shechina* is ailing because our sins. The *Shechina* is ailing because people do not treat each other nicely. When you read these words, pray to G-d that the *Shechina* will rise once again and be healed of its ailing heart (*Tanya, Igeres HaKodesh*, chapter 31, volume 5, p. 244).

Ask yourself, "What can I do to prevent it from ailing in the first place?"

אַתָּה חוֹנֵן לְאָדָם דַּעַת, וּמְלַמֵּד לֶאֱנוֹשׁ בִּינָה. חָנֵּנוּ מֵאִתְּךָ חָכְמָה בִּינָה וָדָעַת. בָּרוּךְ אַתָּה יְיָ, חוֹנֵן הַדָּעַת.

"You graciously, bestow knowledge upon man and teach mortals Your understanding. Graciously bestow upon us, from Your wisdom, understanding and knowledge. Blessed are You G-d, who graciously bestows knowledge."

Ask G-d to fix and engrave inside you the knowledge that you have absorbed in the past day. Ask Him that all this wisdom should be useful to you, and that you should be able to apply it to your life.

הֲשִׁיבֵנוּ אָבִינוּ לְתוֹרָתֶךָ, וְקָרְבֵנוּ מַלְכֵּנוּ
לַעֲבוֹדָתֶךָ, וְהַחֲזִירֵנוּ בִּתְשׁוּבָה שְׁלֵמָה לְפָנֶיךָ.
בָּרוּךְ אַתָּה יְיָ, הָרוֹצֶה בִּתְשׁוּבָה.

Cause us to return, our Father, to Your Law; draw us near, O our King, to Your worship, and bring us back in perfect repentance to Your presence. Blessed are You, O G-d, who desires repentance.

The word *Teshuvah* (repentance) in Hebrew, could also be read as *Tashuv-hey*, "return the letter *hey*." When you repent for your mistakes and sins, you restore the letter *hey* in the name of G-d that was "blemished" through your actions (*Tanya, Iggeres Hateshuvah,* chap. 4, vol. 3, p. 1034).

The two letter hey's in the Tetragrammaton correspond to the different levels of *Teshuvah*. When you do *Teshuvah* out of fear, or because you have sinned, then the first hey is returned. This is *Teshuvah Tata'ah* (lower level *Teshuvah*).

When you desire to elevate yourself and serve G-d in a loftier manner, in order to get closer to Hashem, then the second "Hey" returns. This is *Teshuvah Ila'ah* (Higher level *Teshuvah*).

When you operate at the higher level of *Teshuvah*, your earlier sins are actually transformed to merits.

רְפָאֵנוּ יְיָ וְנֵרָפֵא, הוֹשִׁיעֵנוּ וְנִוָּשֵׁעָה, כִּי
תְהִלָּתֵנוּ אָתָּה, וְהַעֲלֵה אֲרוּכָה וּרְפוּאָה שְׁלֵמָה
לְכָל מַכּוֹתֵינוּ, כִּי אֵל מֶלֶךְ רוֹפֵא נֶאֱמָן וְרַחֲמָן
אָתָּה. בָּרוּךְ אַתָּה יְיָ, רוֹפֵא חוֹלֵי עַמּוֹ יִשְׂרָאֵל.

*Heal us, O G-d, and we will be healed; save us and we will
be saved; for You are our praise. Bring a perfect cure and healing
to all our wounds, for You, Almighty King, are a faithful and
merciful healer. Blessed are You, O G-d, who heals the sick of
Your people Israel.*

At this point pray for those who are ailing physically,
mentally or emotionally. Bring to mind people who you
know that are in need of spiritual healing, too.

תְּקַע בְּשׁוֹפָר גָּדוֹל לְחֵרוּתֵנוּ.

Sound the great shofar for our freedom.

When we reach these words, even though it is not *Rosh
Hashana*, we can recall the Lubavitcher Rebbe's insight that
blowing the *shofar* is symbolic of our speechless cry that
comes from the depths of our heart. We feel no words can
describe our shame for having sinned before Hashem, and
how thirsty we are to be united with His oneness (see *Likutei
Sichos* vol. 4, p. 1146*ff.*).

וְלַמַּלְשִׁינִים אַל תְּהִי תִקְוָה, וְכָל הַמִּינִים וְכָל הַזֵּדִים
כְּרֶגַע יֹאבֵדוּ, וְכָל אֹיְבֵי עַמְּךָ מְהֵרָה יִכָּרֵתוּ, וּמַלְכוּת
הָרִשְׁעָה מְהֵרָה תְעַקֵּר וּתְשַׁבֵּר וּתְמַגֵּר וְתַכְנִיעַ בִּמְהֵרָה
בְיָמֵינוּ. בָּרוּךְ אַתָּה יְיָ, שׁוֹבֵר אֹיְבִים וּמַכְנִיעַ זֵדִים.

*And for slanderers let there be no hope, and let all the
heretics and intentional sinners perish in a moment. Let all the
enemies of Your people be speedily cut off; and uproot, crush,
cast down, and humble the dominion of wickedness speedily in
our days. Blessed are You, O G-d, who breaks the enemies and
humbles the wicked.*

In this section, pause slightly between *ut'mageir*
("crush") and *v'tachnia* ("and subdue"), following the
Kabbalistic idea that *t'akeir ut'shabeir ut'mageir* ("uproot,
break, crush") refer to the three *kelipot* (negative energies)
that must be completely eradicated. *V'tachnia* ("subdue")
refers to *kelipat nogah*, a mixture of negative and positive
energy that must be subdued, but can be purified (*Hayom
Yom*, 26 *Teves*).

שְׁמַע קוֹלֵנוּ, יְיָ אֱלֹהֵינוּ, אָב הָרַחֲמָן, רַחֵם עָלֵינוּ,
וְקַבֵּל בְּרַחֲמִים וּבְרָצוֹן אֶת תְּפִלָּתֵנוּ, כִּי אֵל שׁוֹמֵעַ תְּפִלּוֹת
וְתַחֲנוּנִים אָתָּה, וּמִלְּפָנֶיךָ מַלְכֵּנוּ רֵיקָם אַל תְּשִׁיבֵנוּ.

*Hear our voice, O G-d our G-d. Have mercy upon us,
merciful Father, and accept our prayer in mercy and favor; for*

You are a G-d who hears prayers and supplications. From Your presence, O our King, do not turn us away empty.

Pause at this prayer and take time to mentally make all your personal requests to G-d. Do not be afraid to ask Him about minor details of your life. No detail is too small or too irrelevant to G-d. If it matters to you, it matters to Him.

שִׂים שָׁלוֹם, טוֹבָה וּבְרָכָה, חַיִּים חֵן וָחֶסֶד וְרַחֲמִים, עָלֵינוּ וְעַל כָּל יִשְׂרָאֵל עַמֶּךָ. בָּרְכֵנוּ אָבִינוּ כֻּלָּנוּ כְּאֶחָד בְּאוֹר פָּנֶיךָ, כִּי בְאוֹר פָּנֶיךָ נָתַתָּ לָּנוּ, יְיָ אֱלֹהֵינוּ, תּוֹרַת חַיִּים וְאַהֲבַת חֶסֶד, וּצְדָקָה וּבְרָכָה וְרַחֲמִים וְחַיִּים וְשָׁלוֹם, וְטוֹב בְּעֵינֶיךָ לְבָרֵךְ אֶת עַמְּךָ יִשְׂרָאֵל בְּכָל עֵת וּבְכָל שָׁעָה בִּשְׁלוֹמֶךָ.

Grant peace, welfare, blessing, life, grace, kindness and mercy to us and to all Israel, Your people. Bless us, our Father, all of us, together as one, with the light of Your countenance, for by the light of Your countenance You have given us, O G-d our G-d, the Torah of life, loving-kindness, righteousness, blessing, mercy, life and peace; and may it be fitting in Your eyes to bless Your people Israel at all times and in every hour with Your peace.

The "light of G-d's countenance" can be revealed only when we are united all "as one." But G-d's light cannot enter our lives if there is disunity between us, for "G-d does not dwell in an imperfect, fragmented, place" (*Zohar* 1, 216b).

What, exactly, is G-d's "countenance"?

There are two ways G-d gives your life force to you: "face-to-face" and "behind His shoulders," so to speak. If a person follows G-d's will, His light will flow directly to them, like a friend who gives you a gift face-to-face, with a beautiful smile. If a person doesn't follow G-d's will, He still wants to give His light, but its like "someone who unwillingly throws something over his shoulder" to pay a debt. As you say the words, "Bless us… with the light of Your countenance," think about how you desire to receive light from G-d's face and not his back (See *Tanya, Likutei Amarim,* chap. 22, vol. 1, p. 291).

אֱלֹהַי, נְצֹר לְשׁוֹנִי מֵרָע, וּשְׂפָתַי מִדַּבֵּר מִרְמָה,
וְלִמְקַלְלַי נַפְשִׁי תִדֹּם, וְנַפְשִׁי כֶּעָפָר לַכֹּל תִּהְיֶה.

O my G-d! Guard my tongue from evil and my lips from speaking falsehood. To those who curse me, let my soul be indifferent, let my soul be to all as the dust.

The Sages taught (*Avot* 4:10), *"Be lowly of spirit before everyman."* Some commentators interpret this to mean, "Conduct yourself self-effacingly toward everyman"; that is, "Treat every man with deference, as though he were superior to you."

But the *Mishnah* says *be* lowly of spirit before everyone. It does not tell us merely to *conduct* ourselves as if we were humble. How can you genuinely feel humble in the presence of any other person, even someone who doesn't garner your respect in any way?

The Sages offered us the solution: "Don't judge your fellow man until you have stood in his place." It is his "place"; that is, his environment that causes him to sin. He is influenced by his surroundings. For business purposes, he is forced to absorb some of the world's negative energy. He is presented with tempting situations.

Also it may be his spiritual "place." Evil inclinations come in all shapes and sizes; it could be that this person has a level of temptation that you simply don't have. So "be lowly of spirit before every man." Remember that you are not perfect, you do not have the challenges that other people have, and you do not suffer from the same temptations.

עֹשֶׂה שָׁלוֹם בִּמְרוֹמָיו, הוּא יַעֲשֶׂה שָׁלוֹם
עָלֵינוּ וְעַל כָּל יִשְׂרָאֵל, וְאִמְרוּ אָמֵן:

May He who makes peace on high, make peace on us and on all of Israel, and let us say: Amen.

When you say these words and take three steps back as is customary, remind yourself that in order to make peace in the world you sometimes need to take a few steps back, i.e. to keep yourself humble.

14

Tachnun: Prayers of Remorse and *Teshuvah*

אֱלֹהֵינוּ וֵאלֹהֵי אֲבוֹתֵינוּ, תָּבֹא לְפָנֶיךָ תְּפִלָּתֵנוּ,
וְאַל תִּתְעַלַּם מִתְּחִנָּתֵנוּ, שֶׁאֵין אָנוּ עַזֵּי פָנִים וּקְשֵׁי
עֹרֶף, לוֹמַר לְפָנֶיךָ יְיָ אֱלֹהֵינוּ וֵאלֹהֵי אֲבוֹתֵינוּ, צַדִּיקִים
אֲנַחְנוּ וְלֹא חָטָאנוּ, אֲבָל אֲנַחְנוּ וַאֲבוֹתֵינוּ חָטָאנוּ.

*Our G-d and G-d of our fathers, may our prayers come
before You, and do not turn away from our supplication, for we
are not so impudent and obdurate as to declare before You, L-rd
our G-d and G-d of our fathers, that we are righteous and have
not sinned. Indeed, we and our fathers have sinned.*

Now the heart-wrenching process of real *Teshuvah* (repentance) begins. Ask G-d for forgiveness for past mistakes from the bottom of your heart (*umka deliba*).

Before saying the words of this prayer, contemplate for a moment on the idea of *gevurah mamtik gevurah* ("strength sweetens strength"): you need to fight with strength of what is negative within you. It's a very effective way to break the negative forces (*kelipot*).

In order to break free from the negativity within you, you need to combat back against it with strength. As the saying goes, "fight fire with fire." It's a very effective way to break the negative forces (*kelipos*). As the *Tanya* teaches:

"One should thunder against his animal soul with a strong and raging 'voice' to humble it, arousing the good impulse against the evil impulse. When the light of a Jew's soul does not penetrate his heart, it is merely due to the arrogance of the *sitra achra* (evil side) which will vanish as soon as he rages at it" (*Tanya, Likutei Amarim* ch. 29, vol. 1, pp. 385-6).

Think of a particular negative character trait and say to yourself: "I can't stand when I behave (in an angry manner or _____). I can't stand it when the *yetzer hara* (evil inclination) tricks me."

But don't stay bitter for too long or it will drag you down. The Lubavitcher Rebbe says it should last no longer than what it would take to say five sentences, and then you should shift to more joyous thoughts.

Vidduy / Confession

אָשַׁמְנוּ, בָּגַדְנוּ, גָּזַלְנוּ, דִּבַּרְנוּ דְפִי. הֶעֱוִינוּ, וְהִרְשַׁעְנוּ,
זַדְנוּ, חָמַסְנוּ, טָפַלְנוּ שֶׁקֶר. יָעַצְנוּ רָע, כִּזַּבְנוּ, לַצְנוּ,
מָרַדְנוּ, נִאַצְנוּ, סָרַרְנוּ, עָוִינוּ, פָּשַׁעְנוּ, צָרַרְנוּ, קִשִּׁינוּ
עֹרֶף. רָשַׁעְנוּ, שִׁחַתְנוּ, תִּעַבְנוּ, תָּעִינוּ, תִּעְתָּעְנוּ: סַרְנוּ
מִמִּצְוֹתֶיךָ וּמִמִּשְׁפָּטֶיךָ הַטּוֹבִים וְלֹא שָׁוָה לָנוּ. וְאַתָּה צַדִּיק
עַל כָּל הַבָּא עָלֵינוּ, כִּי אֱמֶת עָשִׂיתָ וַאֲנַחְנוּ הִרְשָׁעְנוּ.

We have transgressed, we have acted perfidiously, we have robbed, we have slandered. We have acted perversely and wickedly, we have willfully sinned, we have done violence, we have imputed falsely. We have given evil counsel, we have lied, we have scoffed, we have rebelled, we have provoked, we have been disobedient, we have committed iniquity, we have wantonly transgressed, we have oppressed, we have been obstinate. We have committed evil, we have acted perniciously, we have acted abominably, we have gone astray, we have led others astray. We have strayed from Your good precepts and ordinances, and it has not profited us. Indeed, You are just in all that has come upon us, for You have acted truthfully, and it is we who have acted wickedly

The *vidduy* (confession) is important because when you sleep, your soul ascends on high, and if you have committed—knowingly or unknowingly—a transgression since your morning prayers, there are heavenly accusers whose job is to block the soul's ascent. As soon as you confess these sins and state your intention never to commit them again, the accusers are silenced and your soul is free to ascend.

The *vidduy* is standardized text of confession and includes every imaginable type of sin (arranged according to the sequence of the *Alef-Beis*), including many things that you will surely have not done. Why should you confess for things you did not do?

Because the people of Israel are one collective soul, so you are confessing for the entire nation (see *Toras Menachem* 5742, vol. 1 p. 100). Another reason is that there might be sins in the list that you yourself have committed unknowingly. Add to the formal list your personal confession of all the errors that you are conscious of having committed.

If you know someone who needs healing in a specific emotional trait, fix it in yourself. If you do *teshuvah* for that person, it will help them.

Confession after the *Amidah*

In Jewish liturgy, confession takes place after the *Amidah*, the standing prayer containing our personal petitions to G-d. Why was this juncture deemed appropriate by the Sages to confess?

Because we needed to prepare ourselves with all the previous prayers so that we are ready to be honest and admit wholeheartedly to Hashem what we have done wrong.

Confession in the Plural

Why are the confessions each phrased in the plural, "We have transgressed, we have acted perfidiously, etc."?

This was done in order not to embarrass us and to avoid making us feel too bad. When we admit we have sinned we know we are not alone and others have made the same mistakes too. This eases the pain, and the path of *Teshuvah*.

יְיָ יְיָ אֵל רַחוּם וְחַנּוּן אֶרֶךְ אַפַּיִם וְרַב חֶסֶד וֶאֱמֶת:
נֹצֵר חֶסֶד לָאֲלָפִים נֹשֵׂא עָוֹן וָפֶשַׁע וְחַטָּאָה וְנַקֵּה:

And the Lord passed before him and proclaimed: L-rd, L-rd, benevolent G-d, compassionate and gracious, slow to anger and abounding in kindness and truth; He preserves kindness for two thousand generations, forgiving iniquity, transgression and sin, and He cleanses.

If you are praying with a Minyan (quorum of ten men) the Thirteen Attributes of G-d's mercy are now said. This was a special formula given by G-d to Moses after

He forgave the Jews for making the Golden Calf. G-d promised that whenever in the future we would need to seek forgiveness, we should recite this formula and it will be effective.

Contemplate each of these special names, how each name is unique and how you can emulate G-d's ways and incorporate these attributes in your own life.

Teshuvah in small doses

"*Teshuvah* is great," the Sages taught (*Yoma* 86a), "for it brings healing to the world." The material world is like a sick person, and a sick person may need to take medication. But only when the exact dosage is administered at exactly the right intervals can medication help.

Taking penicillin all day long would be detrimental. In the same way, crying all day to G-d and feeling bitter about sins would not be productive. You need fresh air too. Be very deliberate and specific about the times you set aside for remorse.

Don't be fooled by the *yetzer hara* that your prayers are "worthless" when you find it difficult to concentrate. The Alter Rebbe teaches (*Tanya, Kuntres Acharon,* p. 308 in Vilna ed.) that as long as at one time during the year you have concentrated on a particular word or prayer, all of your previous efforts that fell short to bring the proper intent to that word or prayer during the year are gathered together and elevated on high to reach Hashem.

Thoughts After *Teshuvah*

After *Teshuvah* you should take a few moments to feel the joy of what you have accomplished. Remember that Hashem is always forgiving, and that nothing stands in the way of our *Teshuvah*. You can feel cleansed, uplifted, and joyful because now, after *Teshuvah*, you have become even more endeared and beloved by G-d. Now you are ready to serve Him with more love and awe. You have greater energy to infuse vitality into all your good deeds.

Repenting for sins you know you will repeat

The *Mishnah* teaches us that we should never sin, planning to repent at a later date. But, the Alter Rebbe adds, when it comes to sins that are almost impossible to avoid, like the sin of neglecting to study Torah for even one minute, it is not the same as saying, "I will sin and repent, sin and repent" (*Tanya, Igeres Ha-Teshuvah* ch. 11, vol. 3, p. 1113)

The important distinction is that you are not using your later repentance as the pretense for the sin. The sin happened almost inevitably. But you still feel bad afterwards because you know it was wrong; so you ask G-d to forgive you.

One may lend this *Teshuvah*—the restoration of his soul to its source—additional strength from the depths of his heart, and likewise add a greater measure of light and joy to the joy of his soul brought on by the *teshuvah*, by comforting his heart from its distress and sorrow, through reflecting with knowledge and understanding, as follows: "Certainly it is true, as said above, that I am utterly remote from G-d, etc.; but it was not I who created myself in a manner that permits the Divine soul to be exiled within the impurity of the body and animal soul. It was G-d who created me so. Why then has G-d done such a thing — to cause [the Divine soul,] a part of His light which fills and encompasses all worlds and before which all is as naught, to descend into [the body], and be clothed in a 'serpent's skin' and a 'fetid drop? Surely this descent must be for the sake of a subsequent ascent. That is, to elevate to G-d the entire animating, animal soul" (*Tanya*, chapter 31, vol. 1, p. 418).

I often give people advice about getting back to praying. Often it is a woman who is now married with children and since she left seminary she has basically dropped her praying. She tries again and again to add prayers to her hectic life but when she fails to see results instantly, she feels disappointed and feels like giving up. "When the kids bother me and don't let me pray, I get more upset with them and then get sad about me being angrier at them."

I remind her that the Land of Israel was not conquered overnight, but step-by-step, over a course of years. So, too, when we try to "conquer" ourselves, it is a process, day by day.

There was once a woman who, as she took stock of the resolutions she had made a year ago, felt discouraged. She saw that despite her hard work, she still had the same flaws that she had had then. She felt that her efforts had been in vain, and she wanted to give up altogether.

She went to talk to her Rebbetzin.

The Rebbetzin sighed and asked, "Do you know how long it takes for a bamboo tree to grow as tall as a building?"

The woman looked at her with a puzzled expression on her face and said, "No, I have no idea."

The Rebbetzin answered the question herself. "After the farmer plants the seed in the ground, he waters and fertilizes it. Only after five years of cultivating the bamboo plant does he begin to see some growth.

"But in the fifth year, the bamboo grows ninety feet in a matter of only six weeks!"

With a warm smile, the Rebbetzin asked: "So now can you answer my question? How long does it take the bamboo tree to grow so high?"

The woman confidently answered: "Six weeks."

The Rebbetzin leaned forward, looked the other woman in the eye, and said gently: "That is your mistake. It takes five years and six weeks. If the farmer would have stopped cultivating the bamboo at any point during those five years, the plant would have died."

She continued, "What was happening during all those years? Underneath the ground an enormous network of roots was developing to support the bamboos sudden growth. Growth takes patience and perseverance. Every step you take makes an impact. You may not see changes right away, but change is happening. With commitment and determination to achieve your goals, and of course with G-ds help, you too will eventually reach great heights."

Another suggestion is simply not to pray when the children are awake. Alternatively, she could try to pray with the children, in song, so that they enjoy it too.

If none of this works, I let her know this passage from *Kuntres HaAvodah* of the Rebbe *Rashab* (pp. 197- 200):

Now, when our meditation is only casual—even though we may become excited and [even] inflamed in our soul or achieve bitterness and a worried heart as mentioned earlier—no change whatsoever takes place in our natural character traits. They appear as strong as ever. That is, after prayer, we will continue with our frivolity and scoffing exactly as before prayer. Or we will indulge our lusts and hedonistic pleasures just as before. Quite the contrary, our natural character traits may be even stronger than before.

There are two reasons for this. The first reason is the joy that we feel in our soul over our excitement and agitation. (This is an experience of *yeshut*, or ego....)

The second reason is that our bitterness and our worried heart lead us to excessive openness of mind (leaving us open to frivolity, scoffing, lust and pleasure even more than before we prayed).

Similarly, if we are hot-tempered and cruel, we will remain the same after this perfunctory *avoda*. We will become angry, have no mercy on our fellow man, and act toward others in a very hardened manner. These traits may become even stronger [than before we prayed], either because of our arrogance [as in the first reason given earlier], or as a result of our bitterness [as in the second reason], which by nature leads to anger.

Those of us who do not fool ourselves and are not too mistaken about ourselves understand well the truth of the matter. We understand how our principal negative character traits (which we have not yet rectified) remain inside of us at full strength without any change. We acknowledge that our *avoda* has not had any effect upon us. And in order to fulfill the supernal intention, for which our soul descended into this world—that being to purify our natural character traits, as described earlier regarding the imperative of doing *avoda* in this world (and all the more so, not to destroy our mission, G-d forbid, by making our natural traits even stronger)—we must agree in our heart to dedicate a fixed hour and proper amount of time to the exercise of prayer.

Our meditation should be specific and detailed. Then every time we meditate on a particular topic, it will become clearer to us and permeate through us. We will become aroused with a true love. In so doing, we will fulfill the *mitzvah* of love of G-d and also fulfill the supreme intention of purifying and refining our own natural character traits. At the same time, we will gain *chayai olam* ("everlasting life of the spirit") with involvement in Torah and *mitzvot*.

15

Chazzan's Repetition of the *Amidah*

After the congregation have recited the *Amidah* (standing prayer) quietly to themselves, the *chazzan* (cantor) repeats the *Amidah* aloud. The original purpose of repeating the *Amidah* was for the sake of those congregants who did not know how to pray themselves. There is a principle in Jewish law that since, "all Jews are guarantors for each other," in many cases one person is able to fulfill a *mitzvah* on behalf of another. So if you are unable to recite the prayers, the *chazzan* can do it for you, and all you have to do is confirm each of the blessings he makes by saying "Amen."

Nowadays we have printed Siddurim in Hebrew and English so everybody is able to pray on their own.

But, *Chasidus* explains, we still continue to carry out the *chazzan's* repetition, not only for the sake of tradition, but because of its powerful spiritual impact.

In addition to saying, "Amen," after each of the blessings, the congregation also makes a further response each time they hear the name of G-d at the end of a blessing: *baruch Hu u'varuch Shemo* ("Blessed is He, and blessed is His Name"). What is the mystical power of this phrase?

"He" refers to G-d's lofty, intangible essence as it preceded the creation process. At that primordial point, G-d has no name or definitive qualities. There is nothing we can say about Him except that "He" is there.

"His name" refers to a later phase in the Chain of Emanation, where G-d has already manifested the different energies that constitute the building blocks of creation. We are not speaking of something quite as high as "He," but it is still a very lofty state that precedes the entire creative process and the world as we know it.

In Hebrew, the word *Baruch* (blessed) also has the connotation of "drawing down" or "disclosing" (see *Torah Ohr, Miketz* 37c). So every time we say *baruch Hu u'varuch Shemo,* we actually bring about a disclosure of an elusive, pristine light, the very essence of G-d and His name that preceded the world!

The repetition of the *Amidah*, then, gives us a wonderful opportunity, as a community to tip the balances of positive energy into the world, by pumping in G-d's light to our souls, bodies and everything else around us. In the words of the Previous Lubavitcher Rebbe, Rabbi Yosef Yitzchak Schneersohn, "For a *chassid*, each of the responses in congregational prayer — such as *amen*, or *baruch Hu u'varuch Shemo* — is a matter of cosmic significance" (*Likutei Dibburim*, vol. 5 pp. 290 -291).

16

Mincha / Maariv

As we engage in the three different services of *Shacharit*, *Mincha* and *Maariv*, besides adding meditations to our prayers, we can focus on the different spiritual flows, called *Sefirot* that shine more brightly at those times.

Each service corresponds to the dominant energy of our Patriarchs, Avraham, Yitzchak, and Ya'akov (See *Brachot* 26b).

The *Shacharit* service is said in the morning as the sun emerges and its light grows, corresponding to the *Sefirah* of *Chesed*, expansive kindness. This service was introduced by Avraham who is famous in the Bible for his many selfless acts of kindness.

During *Shacharit* meditate upon how you want to embody the *Sefirah* of *Chesed* in your life. Visualize yourself in that mode of being, especially in areas in your life that need strengthening.

The *Mincha* service is recited in the afternoon towards sunset, when light is diminishing, corresponding to the *Sefirah* of *Gevurah*, strength and discipline. This prayer service was introduced by the Biblical Patriarch Yitzchak, who was known to serve G-d with *Gevurah*.

As you say *Mincha*, focus on incorporating more discipline into your day, on using your strength to fight the evil inclination. Visualize yourself having the stamina and self-discipline do to all of Hashem's *mitzvot*.

You might also want to think about how beloved *mincha* prayer is to Hashem, because it takes great strength to stop in the middle of a busy day to worship G-d (*Brachot* 6b). He is ever so grateful for your efforts.

The Talmud states, "One must always (*l'olam*) be scrupulous (*zahir*) about the *Mincha* davening" (*Brachot* 6b). "Zahir" can also mean, "illuminate." Rabbi Shneur Zalman of Liadi expounded: When we are careful to pray *Mincha*, it brings a special light to the world, *l'olam* (*Hayom Yom*, 22nd *Adar* I).

The next service, called *Ma'ariv*, (*Arvis*) is recited after dark and corresponds to the *Sefirah* of *Tiferet* (beauty). Something is beautiful when all its component parts are in perfect proportion. This service was introduced by *Ya'akov* whose mode of Divine worship exemplified *Tiferet*, a natural, beautiful balance of *Chesed* and *Gevurah*.

As you pray the Evening Service, try to evaluate whether you are balanced. If not, focus on what areas in our life you need more equilibrium.

17

Shabbat / Yom Tov

There is a tremendous difference between prayers we say during the week and the prayers we say on *Shabbat* and Holidays (*Yom Tov*). To understand why, we need to first learn about the five dimensions of the soul and how they are connected with the different services. They are as follows:

1) *Nefesh*, the "Spirit," which corresponds to the biological life.

2) *Ruach*, the "Breath," which corresponds to the emotional life.

3) *Neshama*, the "Soul," which corresponds to the intellectual life.

4) *Chayah*, the "Life" which corresponds to the transcendental life.

5) *Yechida*, the "Oneness" which corresponds to the Essence.

Through the prayers that we recite every day of the year we are able to be in touch with the first three dimensions of the soul, *Nefesh, Ruach* and *Neshama*. On Shabbat and Jewish Holidays, we tap into the fourth dimension of the soul, the *Chayah*. (This is what the Talmud refers to as the "additional soul" on *Shabbat*. On *Shabbat*, as well as other Holidays, we add an extra prayer called *Mussaf*, the Additional Service, where we gain greater access to the *Chaya* dimension of our soul.) During the *Neilah* prayer of Yom Kippur, the holiest moment of the year, we gain greatest access to the fifth dimension of our soul the *Yechida. Yechida* means Oneness, and at this prayer we are closest to Hashem.

Once you have reached a higher level of soul consciousness at a special time of the year, it does not necessarily mean you have to lose it when the moment passes. Once you tap into a deeper level of the soul, you can continue that "conversation" and access it all the time, so long as you put the work into it. Shabbat and Holidays are not supposed to be times of spiritual elation that dissipate shortly afterwards. The idea is that you access deeper levels of the soul and then maintain that connection.

Rabbi Yosef Yitzchak of Lubavitch relates (*Likutei Dibburim* vol. 4, page 1346): "On Shabbat, my father would pray at considerable length. In those days he used to pray in shul both on weekdays and on Shabbat. He would go there when the congregational prayers began at about 9:30 a.m. When the congregation had finished at about 11:30 a.m. he would begin to say *Baruch She'amar*, completing his private devotions at about 3:00 p.m. or sometimes 4:00 p.m."

"At this age I recall that when I had been a very little boy, I used to run to shul to hear my father at his prayers. At that time, though, my heart was sad: Why didn't my father daven fast like the whole congregation, like my uncles, for example?"

Difference between the Weekday and *Shabbat*

The main focus of our prayer service during the week is to help our G-dly soul overcome the animal soul; and this is a struggle. But the *Shabbat* and holiday prayers have a different focus.

On *Shabbat*, Jewish Law forbids the activity of selecting waste from food (*borer*). This, teaches Rabbi Shalom Dovber of Lubavitch (*s.v. vehu omed* 5663), has a broader, spiritual connotation—it means that the task of "separating" evil from good is not our focus on *Shabbos*. During the week we seek to heal and perfect the world, eliminating evil and replacing it with good, but on *Shabbat* we journey inwards and inhabit a sacred space that is purely good. And the way we pray on *Shabbat* reflects that distinction: During the week we seek the stamina to fight the battles of life, but on *Shabbat* we seek inner peace.

According to the Kabbalah, the good that we do in this world releases trapped sparks of holiness, enabling them to return to their source. On *Shabbat* and on Holidays, we also elevate sparks but the mechanism is slightly different. Just as you go out to work during the week and struggle to succeed, the elevation of sparks on the weekday also involves a battle. The negative forces are heavily invested in keeping that spark trapped and releasing it from captivity takes effort. But on *Shabbat* and the Holidays, an intense spiritual light is drawn down into the world which disarms the negative forces. The sparks are elevated naturally and organically, just by eating, drinking and relaxing; there is no need for a fight (Siddur *Kabbalos Shabbos* from *Zohar Terumah*).

The weekday and *Shabbat* mechanisms do not work independently and are part of one bigger system. The influx of light on the *Shabbat* is only possible due to the work you carry out during the six weekdays; "Whoever toiled before the advent of *Shabbat* will eat on *Shabbat*," the Sages taught (*Avoda Zara* 3a).

Shabbat is also described in the Kabbalah as a "cup." Not only does *Shabbat* receive from the week before—the blessings come pouring in on that day—but these blessings of strength and vitality also get poured into the week ahead.

With this spiritual understanding of the *Shabbat*, the prayers on these days have a fresh significance. G-d has given us a day of rest from engaging in the inner war of personal struggle, and we are rewarded for all our efforts during the week. This is a spiritual freedom that only Hashem can give us, a true present.

The great sage Rav Hamnuna said (*Shabbat* 119b), "He who prays on the Eve of *Shabbat* and says *Vayechulu*, is regarded by the Torah as if he has been made a partner in creation."

In the Talmud, Mar Ukva said, "When a person recites *Vayechulu* the two angels accompanying him place their hands on his head and say 'Your sin is departed and your transgression is forgiven.'"

The *Shabbat* Bride

Shabbat is described in the prayers as a "bride", which has many beautiful connotations. One which is not so well known is the Hebrew grammatical connection between the word bride (*kalah*) and the term *kilayon*, which means to "expire," or to be "consumed," from the verse in Psalms, *kalsa nafshi* ("My soul is consumed"), (*Kuntres Avodah*, p. 221, note 5).

Initially, your soul is found in the barren "wilderness" of physicality, a place devoid of any trace of G-dliness. On *Shabbat* and festivals, G-dliness floods the world, enabling you to escape from this "wilderness." Your soul is aroused during these special times, and she is able to overwhelm and annihilate the negative elements that had entrapped her.

In fact, when we say *vayechulu hashamayim* in the Friday night *Amidah* prayer, two angels come to take away all our sins. We are literally like a bride, totally free of sin! (Rabbi Nisan Mindel, *My Prayer*, vol. 2, p. 64). So when you reach this point, stop and visualize the angels taking away all your sins.

"When a person recites vayechulu in the Friday night prayer, the two angels accompanying him place their hands on his head and say, 'Your sin is departed; your transgression is forgiven'" (*Shabbat* 11b)

Now when *Shabbat* comes and I sing "Come, O Bride (*kalah*)," the realization that the negativity of the week is being consumed because of the prayers and Torah learning I carried out in the week, and my six days of work, I have a bigger smile and still yet more hope for the upcoming week's transformation. All my negativity is burned up!

18

Afterword

Having absorbed all this information, you might easily become overwhelmed by the task at hand. Don't panic! Even if you just read the words in the prayer book with simple devotion you are doing well. That too brings spiritual refinement to the world and orchestrates sublime Supernal Unions above, bringing joy to G-d and to His creation. So try your best to engage your mind and heart in the prayers, but if for whatever reason you are unable, remember that the words of the prayers, composed by prophets and Sages, have tremendous potency.

On his 16th birthday (the 18th of *Elul* 5474/1714) the *Ba'al Shem Tov* found himself in a small village. The local innkeeper had little Jewish education and he hardly knew how to read the prayers, let alone understand what they meant. He was, however, a very G-d fearing individual. On all matters and at all times he would quote the same phrase in the Holy Tongue, "Blessed be He, may He be blessed forever." His wife too would always say in Yiddish, "Praised be His Holy Name." That day, in accordance with the age-old custom of meditating in solitude for some time on one's birthday, the *Baal Shem Tov* went off by himself to the fields. He recited chapters of *Tehillim* and engaged in unifying the Divine names that emanate from its holy verses.

"As I was immersed in this," the *Baal Shem Tov* related, "and unaware of my surroundings, I saw Eliyahu the prophet. There was a smile on his lips. I was taken aback. For when I had been with the *tzaddik* R. Meir, and also when I had been in the company of the hidden *tzaddikim*, I had merited to see Eliyahu, but this was the first time I had merited his appearance while all alone. I wondered about it. And besides, why was he smiling?

Eliyahu said to me, "You are toiling so mightily to have the proper mystical intentions in bringing about the Supernal Unions of the Divine Names that emanate from the verses of *Tehillim*. And Aaron Shlomo the innkeeper and his wife Zlata Rivka know nothing of the unifications that result from his "Blessed be He; may He be blessed forever" and from her "Praised be He and His Holy name." Yet, the Divine harmonies they create resonate in all the heavens more than all the unifications of the Holy Name that are effected by the mystical intentions of the greatest *tzadikim*.

"Eliyahu described to me," the *Baal Shem Tov* continued, "the great pleasure, as it were, that results in heaven from the words of praise and adoration uttered by men, women and children. And most especially, when the praises are offered consistently, for these people are constantly united with G-d in pure faith and with an undivided heart" (*Tanya, Kuntres Acharon* chap. 3, vol. 5, pp. 291-3).

Even if you cannot read the words of prayer properly, G-d will accept your humble offering with love. The *Midrash* teaches on the verse, *v'dilugo alai ahava* ("his omission is beloved to me"), that even if someone inadvertently reads *voyavata* ("and you shall hate") instead of saying *veahavta* ("and you shall love")—"since it came from simple and whole hearted people, it is beloved to me," says Hashem. If you desire a connection with Hashem, you are guaranteed that He will respond to whatever prayers you are able to offer up, even if you mispronounce the words!

There was a man who was never taught how to pray, so he would everyday recite the whole siddur, including all the holiday prayers. The *Baal Shem Tov* visited his town, and when he saw what the man was doing he showed him how to pray in the proper order, slipping papers into his *siddur*. After the man escorted the *Baal Shem Tov* on his way, he noticed that all the papers had fallen out of his siddur to the ground. Dismayed, he mustered up the strength to chase after the *Baal Shem Tov* so that again he would get the proper instruction. As he came closer, this villager saw the *Baal Shem Tov* take a napkin and put it on the river and sailed to the other end of the river without a boat! The villager with his naivete, took his napkin put it on the river and the same miracle occurred for him too. He now approached the *Baal Shem Tov* with trepidation, begging for forgiveness for bothering him once again and asked to be taught once again the order of the prayers.

The *Baal Shem Tov* was almost dizzy with shock. "How did you reach me so quickly?", he asked. The villager answered, I just copied you. I took out my napkin and sailed across the river and here I am.

"If you were able to reach across this river like I was able to," the *Baal Shem Tov* replied, "then just keep on praying just the way you do it now!"

While we prefer to use the *siddur* for our prayers, which was composed by prophets and sages, your own personal petitions to G-d are also sacred. As Rabbi Yosef Yitzchak of Lubavitch commented, "The informal prayers that women are accustomed to whisper before and after candle-lighting, in which they request that G-d light up their home with domestic harmony and with children radiating reasons for joyful satisfaction; the unsophisticated requests that women customarily make before and after they fulfill the *mitzvah* of challah by separating part of their dough, when they ask their family blessed with an ample livelihood so that they be able to support Torah scholars and contribute generously to charitable causes; the homespun prayers that women customarily utter before and after immersion in a mikveh, when they ask to be blessed with fine and healthy children who will grow up to be pious and upstanding men and women. All these customs are Torah."

I pray that this book will help you along this journey of self actualization and redeeming your G-dly soul. I pray that it will help you enjoy the journey towards your inner core.

And always remember what the Talmud teaches: If you make the effort, you will succeed!

Discover the power of prayer and meditation! It gets you to a better place sooner than you can imagine. May Hashem bless you, and enlighten your eyes always. You are reaching new heights!

Appendix A: How Prayer Affects the Chemistry of Your Brain*

The element in the performance of *mitzvos* and the recitation of prayers that lifts them from the mundane into the holy, from the level of "acceptable" to the level of "cherished," is *kavanah*, intention—or, in more contemporary language, mindfulness. Chassidim attempt to copy the specific *kavanos*, intentions, that their Rebbe had in performing a particular *mitzvah*, hoping that by doing so

*Thanks to Yehudis Karbol, who introduced me to the book "Habits of a Happy Brain: Retrain your brain to boost your serotonin dopamine oxytocin and endorphin levels" by Loretta Graziano Breuning, PhD, (Adams Media, 2015) at a Sparks conference, and to Chanie Fetman, who introduced me to Regalena Melrose's "60 Second Fix."

they will be able to duplicate the religious fervor and bliss the Rebbe had attained.

The Torah actually advises us on how to do this. Applying the idea of "mindfulness" to the verse *Ivdu es Hashem b'simchah,* "serve G-d with joy," we can understand it to mean that by serving Hashem, we will find joy. Through the anticipation, fulfillment, connection, and relief of performing *mitzvos,* we come to joy.

Scientists have found that the neurochemical process that leads to joy mimics the stages of *mitzvah* performance. They have isolated four chemicals in the human brain—dopamine, serotonin, oxytocin, and endorphins—involved in the feeling of happiness. Each chemical relates to a different aspect of happiness. Dopamine is activated by anticipation; fulfillment releases serotonin, giving us a feeling of pleasure. Involvement in this pleasure develops oxytocin, which causes a bonding sensation, connecting us intensely with whatever is causing the pleasure. This almost unbearable intensity of emotion releases endorphins, pain relievers, so that the pleasurable act becomes connected in our brains with a sense of escape into joy.

These pleasurable feelings can come from positive sources, such as *mitzvos,* or negative sources, such as harmful substances. Whatever the source, our brains quickly learn to desire more of these chemicals, and habits that lead to happiness are very hard to break.

We can create happy brain chemicals from good habits. This is a powerful tool to relieve stress and gain self-mastery, which leads to healthy self-esteem.

Just as happiness positively affects our whole mind and body, unhappiness negatively affects them. Chronic, unchecked stress actually shrinks the hippocampus, the part of our brain that consolidates memory and that has a part in regulating our emotions and arousal. This decreases our ability to control our emotions, and our functioning becomes mostly reactive instead of reasoned.

How can we create feelings of self-control and self-esteem? How can we combat the sense of powerlessness we may feel, especially when we have overactive, negative emotions? One way is to feel emotionally powerful, successful, and calm—to think ourselves into that. We can visualize ourselves experiencing those states of being, and that visualization leads to a neurochemical response that creates those feelings within us.

The more often we are aware of those calm, positive feelings of inner peace, the longer we are able to sustain them. Our brain appreciates these feelings, and trains itself to recreate them. Let's see how.

Imagine that you are longing to connect with Hashem through prayer. You begin to anticipate all the *brachos* that come to you from starting your day with *tefillah*. As you take your *siddur* (prayerbook), think about what you are about to say, what the words mean, and what you hope to accomplish this day, and you begin to feel good as dopamine is being released. When you begin to say the words, and you consider that you have taken the time to attend to this important activity, you have a real sense of pleasure, which activates serotonin. If you rush through the prayers, though, you will not fully enjoy the sensation, if at all—just as if you quickly eat a cookie you cannot fully possess the pleasure of its taste (only the calories!). It is important to breathe deeply before you begin to pray, to settle your mind. "Intentional breathing is the quickest way to recalibrate the nervous system and shift our bodies from the stress full sympathetic state that dominates the modern life down to the more healing parasympathetic state of being" (Heard from Dr. Tia Trivisonno, ND LAc MSOM, a wholistic nurse practitioner).

While you are praying, you feel yourself connecting to Hashem, and this intense emotion activates oxytocin. As the intensity of bonding reaches a peak, you feel a sense of pain relief, as your endorphins are released, because you realize that Hashem is always there for you, holding you in the warmth of His embrace, and that He will take care of all your needs.

This process can be achieved through any *mitzvah*—learning Torah, preparing your home for Shabbat (the Sabbath), earning money for *tzedakah*, cooking a healthy meal for yourself or others. Any good deed can result in a dose of these happy-brain chemicals, without the need to resort to any unhealthy means.

Praying Can be Relaxing

"Physical relaxation, when practiced daily, brings about an accompanying 'mental relaxation' and a 'relaxed attitude' which enables us to better consciously control our automatic mechanism. Physical relaxation also, in itself, has a powerful influence in "dehypnotizing" us from negative attitudes and reaction patterns"(from *Psycho Cybernetics*, by Maxwell Maltz, MD).

Sing In Jubilation

King David frequently recommends that we sing and dance and make music in our service to Hashem, and many of the verses in *Tehillim* specify what instrument should accompany their recital.

Cheerful music, live or recorded, can have an immediately uplifting effect on us. Whenever practical, music playing in the background as you go about your daily tasks will make them more enjoyable and seem to take less time. If you have musical ability, taking time throughout your day to make music can be uplifting. If you are able to help others create music, that can be an additional source of joy to you.

Singing is also considered making music, and it is known to be spiritually uplifting. The Levites had a duty to sing prayers, morning and evening, in the *Beis Hamikdash/*

Holy Temple. Singing today also includes *davening* with pleasant melodies. Not only does that make it easier to remember the words of the prayers, it also makes it easier to *daven* with feeling and concentration, as you may be more likely to focus on the words and their meanings than usual.

The act of singing is healthful physically and emotionally. Do not let your singing become a source of tension, though, by judging yourself by professional standards (unless, of course, you are a professional singer). You may need to ensure that no one is in the vicinity to hear you, if you are worried that you will disturb others. Sing along to your favorite songs, or make up words as you go along. Pour out your feelings to G-d in song, and you will find yourself describing your worries as joys.

Rabbi Dov Ber Pinson offers the following insight on the connection between singing and davening:

In describing the Levite families' roles in transporting the Tabernacle, the Torah states, "[Moses] did not give [wagons] to the children of *Kehos*, for theirs was the task involving the holy [objects] upon their shoulders to carry."

Why does the Torah state "upon their shoulders to carry"? It could have stated more succinctly, "upon their shoulders." The Talmud explains that the Hebrew word for "carry", *yisa-u* can also mean "to sing," as in the expression *se-u zimra,*' "carry a tune", and therefore the Torah was hinting that the children of *Kehos* were enjoined to sing while they carried the holy articles on their shoulders.

Shemen HaTov suggests a deeper connection between the idea of carrying on the shoulders and singing: After passing successfully through a difficult or dangerous challenge, we feel excited, relieved, and joyful. The *Mishnah* describes such a situation: After Yom Kippur, to celebrate the fact that he had emerged from the Holy of Holies, the *Kohen Gadol* hosted a feast for his friends and relatives. Similarly, the children of *Kehos* were singing in anticipation and celebration of their own success in transporting the *Aron* without mishap.

The Torah is telling us that a person should always sing, even if he is carrying a heavy burden on his shoulders. The singing can ease that burden, and aid in the successful completion of our own personal holy mission.

Praise His Name with Dancing

Dancing is also mentioned in *Tehillim*, as a means of expressing praise and joy.

As a physical exercise, dance is wonderful for getting your heart and blood pumping, keeping your muscles in shape, and clearing your head of worries. Jewish dancing on joyous occasions tends to be done in groups, and the social contact also adds to our happiness. Most dances do not require extensive preparation or expertise, although it is always possible to develop it to higher and higher levels. Just don't go past the level of it being enjoyable.

You should aim for at least a half-hour of dancing at a time, working up from slow to fast to slow, a few times a week. But, if you can only fit in a few minutes at a time, do that.

Other Exercise

If you are unable or currently unwilling to dance, push yourself to add some additional physical exercise in whatever form is available to you: walking up and down stairs, jogging in place, bicycling (outside or stationary), and -calisthenics.

Gardening has the advantages of being gentle while also providing the external beneficial results of beautiful sights, scents, and possibly taste. In addition, if you raise plants or flowers, you have something which you can share with others as gifts.

Replace guilt trips with real ones. Traveling—by foot, bike, car or other means—can provide a quick but long-lasting lift to your physical and mental health, as well as to your spirituality. Visiting places of natural beauty increases our appreciation of and belief in the Creator of the world and his power. *Mah rabu ma'asecha Hashem,* "how wonderful are Your creations, O L-rd!"

Chesed & Tzedakah: Sharing & Caring

Giving of ourselves has a powerfully positive effect on our spirit.

Volunteering our time, effort, or money does not diminish our stock of them but adds to it. We may do these things only because they are *mitzvos* and are required of us, but they can be more beneficial to us than to those we are setting out to help. One excellent technique for improving one's spirits is recommended by many rabbis: Every day, do at least one good deed for someone else that no one knows about. If you can, keep a record of these acts and refer to it once a month, or whenever you are feeling low. The knowledge that you have the ability to help others, that your life has an impact, should lift your spirits.

Practice, Practice, Practice

These ideas cannot help if they are not practiced. To begin, pick the one(s) you are most likely to persevere with, and try to do it a few times a week. Keep a journal—written or recorded—of what, when, where, and for how long. Jot down how you felt when you began and when you stopped.

Referring to this journal can give you insight into what works for you in managing your moods. Also, the act of recording gives many people an outlet for feelings, as you are not restricted to any particular style or limited by time or space. Exercise your freedom of expression!

Meditation and Its Benefits

One way to impress the ideas presented in this book into one's mind is to meditate upon them. Meditation helps us train our brains into beneficial emotional states or behavioral patterns.

Through meditation, a person can come to joy. The Rebbe Rashab teaches:

When we engage in a detailed [and honest] meditation, in order to understand a G-dly concept with our minds, we achieve happiness of the soul, as it is written [in Psalms 113:9] *aim habanim smaicha*, the mother of the children is happy"—(where there is *aim habanim*, (*Binah* or understanding), there is *simchah* (happiness)]. Through detailed meditation, we also come close to G-dliness, from which we derive the greatest amount of happiness in our soul."

The Chassidic almanac *Hayom Yom* (9 Elul) teaches:

Regarding *hitbonenus* (meditation) by profoundly concentrating on a difficult subject, if the matter is of personal concern, then a person will understand it well.... [For] the truth is that when a matter is of personal concern, even those whose minds are weak can strain to attain deep intellectual insights.

In addition, a person who engages in such meditation protects himself against suffering:

"Were it not for Your Torah, which was my rapture (*sha'ashuai*), I would have perished in my suffering." Rabbi Aryeh Kaplan teaches that the word *shasha*—rapture—denotes the serenity and calmness induced by a meditative state in which one utterly divorces oneself from outside troubles, setting up a barrier of spiritual protection against mental suffering.

Meditation On Happiness

Meditations such as the following can be done at any time, in almost any place, to help develop an atmosphere of happiness. Deep breathing and visualizing yourself calm helps to calm down the neural responses of the amygdala, the part of the brain that fires you up into fight and flight mode, allowing you to respond less emotionally to triggering situations.

First, get into a comfortable seated position on a chair that supports your head and arms as well as your back. Your feet should be touching the floor or other support. You may recline slightly, but not so much that you might fall asleep.

Take deep, regular breaths until you are breathing in a steady rhythm.

With each inhalation, visualize that you are breathing in everything that is good: tranquility, love, harmony, and optimism. With each exhalation, breathe out everything that is troublesome: tension, sadness, bitterness, anger, and pessimism.

Feel lighter, as a soothing wave of relaxation [flows over and through] you.

Form your hands into fists until you feel the tension. Count to three. Then slowly open your hands and release the tension. Notice the difference between the tension and the relaxation.

Squeeze your toes tightly, until you feel the tension. After a count of three, relax your toes and release the tension there.

Now tense your forehead, cheeks, and lips. Count to three and release the tension. Reflect on the difference between your previous feelings of tension and your present feelings of relaxation.

Shut your eyes and tighten them. Keeping them closed, relax them, then tighten them again and again relax them.

Finally, tense your back and shoulder muscles. Lift your shoulders up. After counting to three, slowly let them drop as you release the tension.

You now feel completely relaxed. You are so relaxed that you no longer sense the weight of your body.

Now, visualize a white cloud coming closer and closer to you. Its presence is calming. The cloud stops before you, hovering like a magic carpet. You step onto the cloud, and it rises, lifting you up and away. You feel safe and calm and as light as the cloud itself.

You are moving in the direction of a distant site that even from afar is beautiful and majestic. The cloud brings you to the entrance and you step off into the most beautiful surroundings you can imagine. You savor the peaceful colors and beauty, the caressing warmth of the sun shining above.

You are at ease.

This place was made just for you. It is a place to unwind, to connect to the true you.

As you take in the beauty of this place, you notice a sign that reads, This Way to Inner Peace and Happiness. You set out along this path, enjoying the lovely scenery.

Suddenly your way is blocked by a very large boulder. At first you are annoyed. Then you realize that this represents an obstacle in your life that has been preventing you from achieving inner peace and happiness.

You recall a particular situation in your life that has apparently obstructed your happiness. Ponder the details of this situation. As you do, take note of your emotions. Are you sad or angry? Do you feel trapped? Powerless?

Recall that Hashem, Who has given you life, has always been at your side. He has never left you and never will. You have absolute faith that everything that was and will be is for the good of your soul. You say the following: "The events in my life are for the best. This challenge may be an opportunity for me to cleanse, elevate and perfect my soul."

You realize that your struggles with the challenges in your life make it possible for your soul's fiery love for G-d to grow to the point that not even raging waters will be able to extinguish it.

You feel an impulse to push this dirty rock out of your way and out of your life. But then you consider that it might contain something of value.

Instead, you grasp the rock enthusiastically, showing Hashem that you are ready for whatever may be in store for you, that you accept the gift of life with all of its challenges.

Now that you are closer to this boulder, you can see it shimmer. You chip away at the surface dirt, feeling that you are also chipping away your own limitations and ego.

As you work, you understand that you are not a victim of circumstance but an active partner with Hashem, doing the work of bringing G-dliness into the world.

A large chunk of dirt falls away from a crack in the rock, revealing a gem trapped inside the layers.

The rock is too solid, though, and you cannot dislodge the gem. You concentrate now on using your mind, where your Divine soul resides, to transform seemingly negative events into opportunities.

Now that you are thinking this way, you see that if you turn the rock a certain way, the gem will come free. Its brilliance is now completely revealed. Its radiance makes you joyous. You feel the satisfaction of knowing that this jewel belongs to you and that nobody can take it away from you.

This jewel reminds you of your own soul. Hashem has given you a special soul, with everything you need to be complete and happy. No one can take away your happiness unless you allow them to.

This realization was the goal that you had struggled to attain. You now experience the peace of having attained it.

You put the gem in your pocket, and you feel light and free.

This jewel is uplifting. You feel able to soar higher than you had ever dreamed possible, high and close to Hashem, free to worship Hashem as you were meant to, free to love the essence of Hashem, the Good G-d, the Loving Father Who watches over you to make sure that you have everything you need to raise you upward.

Now you can channel this joy into elevating the physical world by performing the *mitzvos*.

Your good deeds create a lively melody. Angels surround you, take your hand and dance with you. With each step you take, you dance higher and higher until you see Hashem's light, radiating joy.

At this point, you have created a means to channel joy into the spiritual and physical realms. Visualize the world as you would like it to be. Pray for what you want.

Ask Hashem to give you what you need in the physical realm to facilitate greater accomplishments in the spiritual realm. Ask Hashem to give you the strength to achieve inner peace so that you can handle challenging situations.

Feel inner peace and happiness.

Now you are ready to bring your new awareness down to earth. The angels at your side are ready to descend with you to help you in your mission. The gorgeous jewel that you carry close to you radiates the light of peace and happiness.

You now descend, accompanied by the angels and this joyous light.

You radiate this new level of joy. Now you are prepared to bring this joy into everything you do, as you perform the *mitzvos* and face your challenges.

You are prepared to share this joy with others. Visualize the people with whom you want to share your joy. Visualize strengthening your bond with them.

You are now touching the ground and you sense the weight of your body. You feel your hands. They are not rigid but open. You think of all the good deeds that they will perform.

You feel your feet that will walk with joy.

You feel your heart calmly beating.

Your voice sounds sweet to your ears.

You sense your face radiating joy; your smile is beautiful and loving, your eyes are shining, your entire being is radiating love and happiness onto others.

Your world is now filled with peace and harmony.

Appendix B: Meditation and Guided Imagery.

The Rebbe *Rashab* teaches, in *Kuntres HaTefilah,* that many people learn Torah but do not change their *middos*, their character traits. Rather, meditative prayer is an effective means of changing one's *middos*. Through deep, focused contemplation on the words of the *tefillos* and their meanings, and on Hashem's wisdom and greatness in conjunction with prayer, Hashem's light is drawn into our mind—and changes the actual physical structure of our brain.

When we are in an emotionally painful situation, our minds tend to negative thought patterns, which increase our pain level. Yet simply by changing these negative thoughts to positive ones, the negative emotion is dissipated and replaced by positive emotion.

Our minds can to be trained to shift thought patterns, so that we can redirect our habitual negative thinking onto more positive paths. Meditation—also called "guided imagery"—is a recognized therapeutic modality that has been used successfully in many settings to benefit patients suffering from a variety of conditions. Research found that not only does meditation have avery powerful effect on one's mental state, but it is actually curative physically as well. Meditation has been shown, for example, to reduce pain and discomfort in seriously injured burn patients as well as in women with metastatic breast cancer, to improve mood in patients suffering from depression and other emotional disorders, to boost the immune response in research subjects, and to speed healing in post-operative patients. Yet medication, the same study found, was only palliative rather than curative, and was effective in alleviating symptoms for only two to three years before the patients developed immunity to it.

Psychotherapist Belleruth Naparstek, a pioneer in Guided Imagery, discusses the effect of imagery on a person's health in her book, *Staying Well with Guided Imagery*. Ms. Naparstek defines "imagery" as any sensory experience—visual, auditory, olfactory, gustatory, or tactile—of which we retain a memory. She explains:

"This is the first operating principle of imagery: Our bodies don't discriminate between sensory images in the mind and what we call reality. Although images don't have the same

intense impact on the body that real events do, they elicit the same essential quality of experience in the body. It's a little bit like what an echo is to the sound that generated it, or perhaps a pastel version of bold original colors. With sensory image, echoes of the mood, emotions, physiological state, and blood chemistry associated with the original event reverberate in the body.... We can deliberately introduce healthful images, and the gullible body will respond as if they, too, were approximations of reality. Research findings show the physical changes that can occur in the body as a result of such engineering with the imagination...."

"The second key principle that makes guided imagery work is this: In the altered state, we are capable of more rapid and intense healing, growth, learning, and change.... By altered state, I mean a relaxed focus, a kind of calm but energized alertness, a focused reverie. Attention is concentrated on one thing or a very narrow band of things."

Additionally, research by Dr. Sara Lazar of Harvard University over a 30-year period showed a thickening (indicating strengthening) in the cortex of those subjects who regularly engaged in meditation—the very opposite of what typically happens as the brain ages. (The cortex of the brain is the area thought to be involved in integrating emotional and cognitive processes, and aging is associated with thinning of the cortex.)

Dr. Lazar interviewed these subjects and found that compared to the control group, they possessed greater mastery over their emotions and experienced a lower susceptibility to emotional imbalances such as anxiety or depression, and to age-related ailments such as dementia, Alzheimer's, and Parkinson's disease.

Clay Routledge, Ph.D. presented "five scientifically-supported benefits of prayer":

Prayer improves *self-control,* because "self-control is like a muscle", which can become tired from overuse, but also can be strengthened through proper training. Research indicates that praying properly strengthens self-control.

Prayer makes you *nicer*—researchers found that people who prayed for others in need, responded less aggressively to provocation.

Prayer makes you more *forgiving*—researchers found that people who prayed on behalf of their spouse or friends were more likely to forgive them.

Prayer increases *trust*—people who prayed together with a close friend reported increased feelings of unity and trust. (And close friendships tend to develop between people who pray together regularly.)

Prayer is a *stress reliever*—researchers found that "praying for material gain did not counter the effects of stress," but "the focus on others" was seen "to be contributing to the stress-buffering effects of prayer." In other words, selfish prayer "does not positively influence well-being and may even harm it", while prayers of thankfulness or praise "has a positive effect on mental well-being."

If secular meditation can have such a positive effect on our brain, then certainly infusing our mind with holy thoughts will change our brain structure for the better, resulting in improvements in our emotions and actions. And then we will reach new heights!

Appendix C: Digging Wells.

In *Words of the Living G-d: Selected Discourses from Rabbi Zalman of Liadi's Classic Torah Or* (adapted by Rabbi David Wagshal), the Alter Rebbe offers illuminating commentary on each *parshah*, revealing the deeper meaning of the deceptively simple sentences that—like every aspect of the Torah—are still relevant to us today.

Parshas Toldos teaches us enormous lessons about prayer. It describes how our forefather Yitzchak found water: *"Yitzchak dug again the wells of water which they had dug in the days of [his father] Abraham, which had been filled up by the Philistines .... The servants of Yitzchak dug in the valley and found there a well of living water"*—that is, a source of continually flowing, gushing water.

This source originates in the Garden of Eden, as the Torah tells us, *"A river went forth from Eden to water the garden."* This river divided into four branches, and the fourth was named Pras. The Talmud tells us that the river Pras is an underground water table that is the source of all the water in the world. When one digs and reaches the water table, he has reached the river Pras.

We can access the original Eden, via Pras, by digging wells and catching the water that gushes forth. This is not, however, only about the physical water that sustains our physical life, but about the "living water" that sustains our spiritual life as well.

Prayer is likened to digging wells. Learning Torah after we pray is like filling up our well with the living waters. Our *mitzvos* enable us to "drink" from the well that we dug and filled up, and "hydrate" our soul from the living waters of Torah. Once received, this essential boost will help us flow like a river in our service of Hashem.

Imagine having a $1000 bottle of wine. (Yes there is such a thing.) Then imagine that wine being poured directly into your cupped hands; the wine keeps flowing, but your hands are not able to contain the precious liquid.

God is pouring and pouring his Godliness into us, but we need to create a vessel to contain it.

The vessel is our prayers.

Hashem is sending us a message of encouragement: He will fill our wells, but we have to dig them! Pray sincerely, and learn Torah afterward, and a river of G-dly help will flow from Eden and fill up the wells that we have dug. Learning Torah without praying sincerely will not create a vessel large enough to receive all the G-dly energy He wants to give us.

There is another message to us in the *pasuk* in *parshas Vayeitzei*, "*Vayashkeim Lavan baboker*, Lavan woke up early in the morning" to greet Yaakov. Lavan, Yaakov's father-in-law, represents the "whiteness" of Hashem, the thirteen Divine attributes and this teaches us that the best time to "catch" this flow at its fullest, is in the morning.

"The morning prayer service is designed to bring out the natural love of a Jew for G-d, and the desire to do only His will, even in abnegation of one's own desires. This feeling is augmented by a period, whether brief or prolonged, of Torah study immediately after prayer, so that one can go about one's business throughout the day."

Often, we get so wrapped up in our daily business that the reservoir of spirituality, the well that we dug in the morning becomes stopped up. Yet every little *mitzvah* we do taps into that wellspring, and we can draw from it to nourish and quench the dehydration of our souls. Through our daily prayers, we develop the ability to draw from that spiritual essence. After we have expended effort of praying and learning, we will be able to draw from those living waters to unite with Hashem through His Torah, and gain true sustenance—physical and spiritual—from the only Source.

Appendix D: Holistic Treatments and Practitioners

Progress in healing may take time (depending on different variables, such as bad diet, severity of trauma, lack of social support *etc.,*) and for that reason I have found these therapies to help speed up the healing process of mind body and soul.

(Many times just changing a persons diet has alleviated or even eradicated emotional disorders. For example eliminating sugar, going on a gluten-free diet and not over eating).

Provided here is a brief summary about these wholistic treatments and the practitioner's contact information.

Emotion Code — **Rabbi Kaplan, (347) 765-0770**

WHAT IS EMOTION CODE?

DR. BRADLEY NELSON ON KSL-TV

The Emotion Code is a powerful and simple way to rid your brain from of unseen baggage, *I.e,* from past traumas. Releasing trapped emotions often results in the sudden disappearance of physical problems, self-sabotage, and recurring relationship difficulties. (Using laser lights and or magnets.)

Somatic Therapy — **Chani Fetman, (347) 534-6474.**

There is an approach that accesses our thoughts through our bodies' physical sensations called self-regulation training —otherwise known as somatic healing. We can not think ourselves into that. We all desire, balance, focus, and vigor. The good news is that we need nothing external, only what is inside of us for self-actualization, happiness and passion. It all starts with accessing the natural ebb and flow in the nervous system through self-regulation. All changes need self-regulation to be sustained. Self-regulation training, *i.e.,* feet on the ground breathing, feeling the support of the area we are on, lowers blood pressure and heart rate and relaxes muscles and supports fullness of life.

When we are in this state the parasympathetic branch of our nervous system is dominant. If we are stressed our amygdala primal brain chooses fight flight or freeze reaction. The amygdala is served with physical sensation. If we want quicker approach and a deeper and lasting result, we need an approach based on sensations.

NAET — Dr Binyamin Delfiner, (718) 839-0346

NAET balances the 12 energy channels (acupuncture meridians). With regard to various substances (foods, chemicals, environmental), or emotional charges and allows the energy channels to remain free flowing.

Cranio-Sacral — Rochel Schapiro, (917) 373-4870

Cranio-Sacral is a gentle, hands-on holistic healing method that releases tensions deep in the body to improve emotional health, physical well-being and whole-body performance. CST has gained its popularity for effectively relieving its clients from anxiety and stress related symptoms, headaches, insomnia, fatigue, chronic pain, hormone imbalances and many other health concerns. Its gentle approach offers a relaxing pleasant experience for all ages.

EMDR — Aliza Horowitz, (718) 730-3850

Eye movement desensitization and reprocessing (EMDR) is a form of psychotherapy developed by Francine Shapiro that emphasizes the role of distressing memories in some mental health disorders, particularly posttraumatic stress disorder (PTSD). It is an evidence-based therapy used to help with the symptoms of PTSD. It is thought that when a traumatic or distressing experience occurs, it may overwhelm normal coping mechanisms. The memory and associated stimuli are inadequately processed and stored in an isolated memory network.

EMDR therapy is as effective as cognitive behavioral therapy (CBT) in chronic PTSD.

The goal of EMDR is to reduce the long-lasting effects of distressing memories by engaging the brain's natural adaptive information processing mechanisms, thereby relieving present symptoms. The therapy uses an eight-phase approach that includes having the patient recall distressing images while receiving one of several types of bilateral sensory input, such as side to side eye movements. EMDR was originally developed to treat adults with PTSD; however, it is also used to treat trauma and PTSD in children and adolescents.

EFT — Sara Tova Best, (917) 557-5938

E.F.T. (Emotional Freedom Technique) focuses on negative self- talk and deletes energetic body memories to provide a space for positive and permanent change.

E.F.T. is based on the principles used in acupuncture—but without the needles. The client (1)mentally 'tunes into' specific emotions and issues; (2)while stimulating certain meridian points in the body (by tapping on them with their fingertips). EFT has been reported successful in thousands of cases covering a huge range of emotional, health and performance issues. It often works where nothing else does.

Feldenkrais — Tzvia Rosenthal, (718) 310-8679

The Feldenkrais Method is a type of exercise therapy devised by Moshe Feldenkrais (1904–1984). The method is claimed to reorganize connections between the brain and body and to improve body movement and psychological state.

Nuero Feedback — Sara Benamou, (786) 657-9155

Neurofeedback is direct training of brain function, by which the brain learns to work more efficiently. Based on electrical brain activity, Neurofeedback is training in self-regulation, which allows the system (the central nervous system) to function better.

Neurofeedback addresses problems of brain disregulation, including anxiety-depression spectrum, attention deficits, behavior disorders, various sleep disorders, headaches and migraines, and emotional disturbances. It is also useful for organic brain conditions such as seizures, the autism spectrum, and cerebral palsy and more.

One Brain — (in Monsey) Mordechai and Bracha Shiner, (845) 354-4456

One Brain is a noninvasive energetic stress release method. Together with muscle testing we release blocked or stagnant energy caused by emotional stress or trauma including stress that has accumulated even from in utero. We have experience helping people with fears, bedwetting, nervousness, birth issues (including fears of birth or breach) and any of the wide variety of issues that come as a result of emotional stress.

Acupuncturist — Claudine Amirian, (917) 309-2758

Lac, Mstom, Licensed Acupuncturist, Herbalist and healer, has a BS in Psycology and nutrition from NYU and a masters in Oriental medicine and health, science and herbology. She has been a student of Miriam's Tanya classes and has incorporated some of the meditations in her healing work. Claudine practices Chinese medicine which assists the body to naturally heal. Chinese medicine is a holistic medicine that activates the bodies Qi and promotes natural healing by enhancing recuperative power, immunity and physical health. Claudine specializes in treating women and children with balancing hormones, boosting fertility, pain management and more.

Acupuncture and Chinese Medicine — Esther Hadassah Simons, (718) 774-1037

Nutritionalist — **Jenia Yashaya, (516) 669-1019**

Licensed as a Holistic Health Coach from the Institute of Integrative Nutrition where the true meaning of health and happiness was learned. She had a B.S. degree in Nutrition Therapy & Exercise Physiology. She also became a Board Certified Holistic health Practitioner, from the American Association of Drugless Practioniners as well as a member of The International Association for Health Coaches. Drawing on this knowledge, Jenia can help her clients create a completely personalized roadmap to health that suits their unique body, lifestyle, preferences, and goals.

"You are given only one body and mind. Of all the things you try to achieve and possess in this life, your health should be your first priority. I find it ironic that, in general, people take better care of material possessions than themselves. Nothing makes her happier than to see her clients feel good after she has helped educate and motivate them to accomplish their health goals and quality of life. Happiness for her lies in the ability to change someone's life from the inside out!

Jenia is so passionate about holistic health that she now works with whole food supplements in a mission to get as many people in the world as naturally healthy as possible.

EMDR specialist — Devora Kozlik, (347) 631-7003

About the Author

Miriam Yerushalmi holds an M.S. in Psychology and Marriage and Family Counseling. Trained at Pepperdine University (graduation 1990). Miriam works in private practice with families and children, including volunteering many hours providing a resource for the neediest to access appropriate Mental Health care.

Miriam is uniquely skilled at combining behavioral and humanistic approaches to address a wide spectrum of psychopathology. From panic disorders to addiction to depressive disorders, anxiety, anger management and ADHD, Miriam imparts self regulation techniques where clients learn to develop tools for a balanced and fulfilled life.

Miriam is a sought after speaker who lectures internationally and has over 250 audio classes available. She writes regularly for the Jewish Press, lectures for Torah Anytime and has presented workshops at the annual *Nefesh* conference for therapists. Since 2014 she began working for SPARKS as a counselor, in addition giving teleconferences and webinars on the topic of overcoming stress and anxiety as well as writing articles for their magazine called "True Balance" and other duties. She continues to teach a weekly class in the central synagogue in Crown Heights, NY (770) as well as in Long Island, each of which started over 15 years ago.

Miriam Yerushalmi fuses essential Torah principles with her background in Mental Health to empower individuals to release their inner healing potential while aligning with life's purpose on essential life issues, ranging from relationships and parenting to self improvement.